THE GOOD SOLDIER

How to Fight Well,

Finish the Race,

and Keep the Faith

GREG AMUNDSON

THE GOOD SOLDIER

How to Fight Well, Finish the Race, and Keep the Faith

ISBN 978-0-578-58236-8

By Greg Amundson

3703 Portola Drive, Santa Cruz, CA 95060

www.GregoryAmundson.com

Edited by Patti Bond

Layout and Design by Brooktown Design, www.brooktown.com

Illustrations by Joseph Carlos Fitzjarrell, www.fitznice.com

The author has done his best to articulate and illustrate God's Word by means of prayer, meditation and contemplation. Italics or brackets within a Scripture are the author's own emphasis.

Published by:
Eagle Rise Publishing, Virginia Beach, VA.
EagleRisePublishing.com

Printed and bound in the USA and UK on acid-free paper.
Additional books can be purchased through Amazon.

PRAISE FOR THE WORK OF GREG AMUNDSON

"Greg Amundson is a true warrior leader and monk. His deep commitment to his faith, and ability to communicate that faith through his passion for the warrior mindset, is unparalleled. *The Good Soldier* is another lighted path that Greg has provided for those searching for Truth."

— ***Mark Divine***, U.S. Navy SEAL (Retired) *New York Times* bestselling author of *The Way of the SEAL, Unbeatable Mind* and *Staring Down the Wolf*

"Greg's ability to transcend boundaries and speak to the essence of spirituality is profound and encouraging."

— ***Scott McEwen***, #1 *New York Times* bestselling co-author of *American Sniper*; national bestselling *Sniper Elite* series, and the new *Camp Valor* series of novels

"I often tell people at my seminars, 'We don't need more Buddhists in the world, we need more Buddhas. We don't need more Christians, we need more Christ-like beings.' And such is the case with my amazing, breathing brother Greg Amundson. He's not one of those wishy-washy, praise the Lord, in-your-face, superficial Christians: He is a former SWAT Operator, DEA Special Agent, U.S. Army Captain, and CrossFit athlete and coach. He is a spiritual warrior, and he carries God in his heart. Greg's sermons, lectures and books teach the principles of spiritual development that can change your life."

— ***Dan Brulé***, world renowned lecturer and international bestselling author of *Just Breathe*

"Greg Amundson is the epitome of a modern day warrior. He leads in all aspects of his life: as a warrior, as a Christian, and as a fitness expert. He writes with magical simplicity, yet is rigorous in his research and reasoning. As a leadership and motivation coach, when I need my own motivation I look to Greg Amundson. His track record of proving the validity of his message in his own life, and the lives that his message touches, is astounding."

— ***Jason Redman***, Navy SEAL (Retired) and *New York Times* bestselling author of *The Trident: the Forging and Reforging of a Navy SEAL Leader*

"Greg Amundson is one of the most prolific author's and speakers of our time, and his work will profoundly bless your life."

— ***Dr. Gabrielle Lyon***, DO, Special Operations, Task Force Dagger

"Greg Amundson's new book *The Good Soldier* contains a visionary message on leadership, self-mastery, and walking the path of a modern day warrior. This is a profound and encouraging read that has reinvigorated my desire to be of service to others. Hooyah!"

— ***Joe De Sena***, Spartan Founder & CEO and #1 *New York Times* bestselling author of *Spartan Up!*

"Greg Amundson has the ability to weave the warrior mindset and biblical message in a way that cuts to my heart. His sermons and books encourage me to put God first, strive for self-mastery, and be of greater service to others."

— ***Jay Dobyns***, ATF Special Agent (Retired) *New York Times* bestselling author of *No Angel* and *Catching Hell*

ALSO BY GREG AMUNDSON

Published Books

Your Wife is NOT Your Sister – (And 15 other love lessons I learned the hard way)
Robertson Publishing – 2012

Firebreather Fitness – Work Your Body, Mind and Spirit into the Best Shape of Your Life
(with TJ Murphy) Velo Press – 2016

The Warrior and The Monk – A Fable About Fulfilling Your Potential and Finding True Happiness
Robertson Publishing – 2018

Above All Else – A Year of Increasing Wisdom, Stature, and Favor
Eagle Rise Publishing – 2018

Victory! – A Practical Guide to Forging Eternal Fitness
Eagle Rise Publishing – 2019

CrossFit® Journal Articles

A Chink in My Armor

Coaching the Mental Side of CrossFit

CrossFit HQ – 2851 Research Park Drive, Santa Cruz, CA.

Diet Secrets of the Tupperware Man Vol. I

Diet Secrets of the Tupperware Man Vol. II

Forging Elite Leadership

Good Housekeeping Matters

How to Grow a Successful Garage Gym

Training Two Miles to Run 100

ACKNOWLEDGMENTS

First and foremost, I am deeply grateful for the everlasting love and embrace of God and His Son, Jesus Christ. For my beloved parents, Raymond and Julianne Amundson, who encouraged me from a young age to develop my mind, body, and spirit in such a manner that I could be of greater service to others. A great deal of appreciation is extended to Brooklyn Taylor for her brilliant layout and design contributions to this book. I am also indebted to the plank owners of the Patriot Authors Network and Eagle Rise Speakers Bureau: Robert Vera, Josh Mantz, Jay Dobyns, Jason Redman, Kevin Briggs, and Karen Vaughn. Your true "Warrior Monk" spirit continues to inspire me more every day. Finally, to the great mentors whose leadership has deeply influenced my life: Greg Glassman, Mark Divine, Dan Brulé, Londale Theus, Ken Gray, Chaplain Richard Johnson, Pastor Dave Hicks, Dr. Deepak Chopra, Dr. Suhas Kshirsagar, Raja John Bright, Dr. Gary Tuck, Dr. Steve Korch, Baba Hari Dass, and Pastor René Schlaepfer.

SYMBOLISM

—◆◆◆◆—

"God is your protecting shield and your triumphant sword."

—Deuteronomy 33:29

THE GOOD SOLDIER

DEDICATION

*"Children, obey your parents in everything,
for this pleases the Lord."*

— Colossians 3:20

*This book is dedicated in loving memory
to my mom and dad, who provided me with the greatest
example of a "Heart like Christ" I have ever known.*

*"God is more worthy of your pursuit, attention, and love than all
the other passions of the world combined."*
— Dr. Raymond Amundson

"God is entirely devoted to your personal advancement."
— Julianne Amundson

A NOTE TO THE READER

For the purposes of this book, I will interchangeably use the terms *warrior*, *spiritual warrior*, and *biblical warrior*. Although the term "spiritual warrior" is becoming increasingly popular in secular circles, I remain adamant that the noblest revelation of the warrior archetype is found in the Holy Bible, and that the highest expression of our understanding for all matters of spirituality must also be in accordance with the Word of God.

In this context, *spiritual warfare* is an engagement with an enemy force that retains its headquarters in the supernatural realm, although the effects are experienced in the natural world. As the Apostle Paul explained, *spiritual warriors* battle against the "powers of this dark world [i.e., the natural world] and against the spiritual forces of evil in the heavenly realms [i.e., the supernatural realm]" (Ephesians 6:12).

Greg Amundson

Santa Cruz, California, 2019

TABLE OF CONTENTS

FOREWORD

THE POWER OF LEADERSHIP

THE POWER OF LEADERSHIP

FOREWORD BY JASON REDMAN

In 2016 a friend of mine told me about a real-life warrior poet. A man who was not only a warrior, but who also lived the warrior ethos in all aspects of his life. He was a law enforcement officer, an Army officer, a founding athlete of CrossFit, a business owner, an author, a high-level practitioner of multiple martial arts, and a steadfast Christian. When I heard about this amazing individual, I wondered what he would be like in person when I met him; a cross between Arnold, Jesus, Robo-Cop, the Rock, and Bruce Lee.

Several months later I met Greg Amundson in person. He was all the things my friend described and more. He had an amazing positivity about him that put you at immediate ease. He had a boundless encouraging energy that made you walk away feeling better about yourself. Only a few years later I would define the balance in how Greg lives as the Pentagon of Peak Performance. The Pentagon of Peak Performance includes five key areas that modern day warriors must develop to be ready for any attack that may come their way; whether the attack is physical, mental, or even spiritual.

The five areas of the Pentagon are Physical Leadership, Mental Leadership, Emotional Leadership, Social Leadership, and Spiritual Leadership.

Over the last several years I have had the honor to spend time with, work out with, hang out with and even worship with Greg Amundson. He truly is one of the most perfectly balanced people I know and he lives the Pentagon of Peak Performance every day. Greg recently reached out to me with a humble request: to write the foreword for his new book, *The Good Soldier*. As I read through the book, I was reminded once again that being a good soldier and warrior is synonymous with being a good leader. Sadly, many people that want to be a modern-day warrior fail to understand the path of leadership and discipline that goes with it.

I've learned that leadership is not the position that you hold or the rank that you wear on your collar. It is not the amount of money you have in your bank account. It is not the car you drive. It is none of that. It is how you carry yourself. It is how you project optimism. It is how you prepare yourself for the unexpected things that may never happen, but could. It's how you motivate people regardless of how you feel.

It is a resolute confidence in the darkest storms and how you lift others out of the darkness. It is the things you do day in and day out that make people say, "I want to follow that individual."

Once you choose the path of warrior and leader, then you must commit to lead always. So many people want to pick and choose when they lead. I made this mistake when I was a younger leader. It was almost to the detriment of my own career. Leadership is leading at all times in all situations. It is leading your family. It is leading in your community. It is leading your business. And most importantly, it is about leading yourself.

As I read through the book and Greg's correlations between Scripture and being a warrior, I could not help but recognize the power of Greg's life. The discipline and self-leadership that Greg maintains in his life is inspiring. In addition, the balance that Greg has achieved in each area of the Pentagon of Peak Performance can be an example and motivation for you to do the do same. Greg Amundson is indeed the good soldier.

The highest level of the Pentagon is Spiritual Leadership. Most people either intentionally or through ignorance neglect this. Greg Amundson makes it the focus of this book because he understands the power it holds to become the highest level of warrior leader. The greatest leaders and warriors have always understood this. I have witnessed it and felt it firsthand on the battlefield. And the Bible gives countless examples of great warriors embracing the Holy Spirit to overcome impossible odds.

Iron sharpens iron. It is time to hone your spiritual leadership and become the good soldier, and this book will teach you how.

Lead Always and Overcome All,

Jason Redman

U.S. Navy SEAL (Retired)

New York Times bestselling author of *The Trident* and *Overcome*

PREFACE

AFTER GOD'S OWN HEART

PREFACE

"Join with me in suffering,
like a good soldier of Jesus Christ."
— 2 Timothy 2:3

"I have fought the good fight, I have finished the race, I have kept the faith."
— 2 Timothy 4:7

—♦♦♦♦—

THE LORD IS STILL LOOKING, as He was during the time of King David, for men and women after His own heart.[1] This book is designed to be a spiritual and intellectual journey that will enable you to relate to yourself as a victorious warrior and leader. In other words, this book will strengthen your heart.

God wants you to have a strong heart. However, when the Bible speaks about "heart," it is not the cardiopulmonary organ beating within your chest. Nor is it the whimsical Valentine's Day heart on Hallmark cards. The heart in the Bible refers to the deeply rooted, ingrained, and habitual ways of thinking that shape your entire life. For this reason, having a "change of heart" is far superior to a mere "change

---

[1] The book of Acts records the ever-inspiring Word of God: " I have found David the son of Jesse to be a man after my own heart" (Acts 13:22).

of mind." Thoughts and emotions are like tides of the sea—they ebb and flow, and they come and go. However, a "heart after God" is equatable to a mighty fortress in which the weary take refuge and shelter.

God is always more concerned with the *person you are becoming* than the *things you are doing*. And the person you are becoming will be either severely limited or abundantly blessed depending on your thoughts about God. The Bible says, "Although people look at the outward appearance, God looks at the heart."[2] This means that the most important fact about you is not what you do at a particular time (*the outward appearance*), but rather what, deep in the recesses of your mind, you conceive God to be like (*the heart*).

By the mysterious law of *creation*, you tend to move in the direction of your privately held mental image of the *Creator.* Being made in the image of God, every facet of who you are *connects* you to God, and every facet of who you are *reflects* God to those around you. It is imperative that these *connections* and *reflections* of God correspond as closely as possible to the true being and nature of God.

---

[2] 1 Samuel 16:7

If history is evidence of human nature, then your actual ideas about God may very well be inconsistent with His true Being as recorded in His Word and revealed by His Son. For example, the Bible is full of descriptions of people who thought God was other than who He actually is.[3] These people substituted for the true God an image based on their own misconception of Him.[4] Only a brief and honest recollection of your life would demonstrate that it becomes increasingly difficult to think rightly about yourself when you are not thinking rightly about God, and relating correctly to Him.[5]

One of the fantastic archetypes of the Old Testament biblical record was that of the *warrior*. And in the New Testament account, the Apostle Paul did not arbitrarily settle on metaphors and illustrations of *soldiering, armor, swords, racing,* and *leading* when teaching his doctrine.[6] These examples empower the reader to identify with the personal qualities of courage, determination, resilience, and unequivocal faith in God.

---

[3] Ref; Romans 1:21-25

[4] Ref; Exodus 32:1-8

[5] I am deeply indebted to the brilliant mind of the Christian Mystic A.W. Tozer and his book *The Knowledge Of The Holy* (New York, NY. Harper Collins, 1961) for helping me frame and conceptualize the ideas in this and the preceding paragraph. Refer to the endnote section for more information on his work.

[6] Ref; 2 Timothy 2:4, 4:2, 4:7; Ephesians 6:10-17

To cultivate a heart for God means that you think rightly about God, and that you think rightly about yourself. This book will empower you to see yourself as a warrior and a leader. Furthermore, this book will shape within your mind the idea that God is good, devoted to your spiritual advancement, and desirous of enabling you to lead yourself and others.

I pray that the ideas in the following pages will inspire you to be a *good soldier* and that you would *fight well, finish the race, and keep the faith.*[7]

— GREG AMUNDSON

---

[7] 2 Timothy 4:7

PART ONE

HOW TO FIGHT WELL

THE WARRIOR GOD

"The LORD is a warrior."
— Exodus 15:3

"I am a warrior and a member of a team."
— U.S. Army Soldier Ethos

COMMENCING WITH THE OLD TESTAMENT and marching through the entire recorded historical account of the Bible, illustrations and examples of the warrior archetype and spiritual warfare are themes of resounding importance for the follower of Jesus Christ. In fact, for you to faithfully obey the covenant commands established through the ministry of Jesus, the archetype of the warrior will be both sufficient and necessary for you to fully understand and relate to. *Sufficient* in that through the establishment of a spiritual warrior's mindset and acceptance of "the full armor of God"[8] you would be equipped to defeat the fiery attacks of evil and temptation. *Necessary* in the realization that "the Son of God appeared for this purpose—to destroy the works of the

[8] Ref; Ephesians 6:14-17

devil."[9] Descending from the heavens above, Jesus Christ employed the most sophisticated special operations mission of all time. Jesus courageously "closed with and destroyed the enemy,"[10] and through his example invited everyone who would follow him to do the same.

Through a careful examination of spiritual warfare and the archetype of the warrior in the Old and New Testaments, we will investigate the progressive development of large-scale warfare, from the tense arena of single combat to the ultimate, close-quarters battlefield for our very heart and mind. Therefore, the theme of spiritual warfare, in particular the battlefield techniques and strategies employed by Jesus Christ, will be of immense importance for all those who seek to experience "a spirit of wisdom and revelation in the knowledge of God."[11]

---

[9] 1 John 3:8
[10] Hebrews 2:14b. Reference creed of the U.S. Army Solider
[11] Ephesians 1:17

LARGE SCALE WARFARE

"'Not by might nor by power, but by my Spirit' says the LORD Almighty."
— Zechariah 4:6

AS WE BEGIN OUR INVESTIGATION of the biblical warrior and spiritual warfare, let us turn our attention to the book of Judges and Gideon's victory over the Midianites.[12] In this particular battle, three observations of immense importance are immediately brought to our attention:

1. *The biblical warrior was not reliant upon the support of a large army.*
2. *The biblical warrior's victory was not achieved with sophisticated weaponry.*
3. *The biblical warrior was absolutely dependent upon God.*

---

[12] For the purposes of this book, I will interchangeably use the terms *spiritual warrior* and *biblical warrior.* Although the term "spiritual warrior" is becoming increasingly popular in secular circles, I remain adamant that the noblest expression of the warrior archetype is found in the Holy Bible, and that the highest expression of our understanding for all matters of "spirituality" must also be in accordance with the Word of God.

At first glance, God's battle plan may seem counter-intuitive to the precepts of modern warfare. After all, the Bible is full of examples of God calling His people into engagements against a superiorly numbered force that is armed with more sophisticated weapons and the advantage of greater military training. However, this seemingly senseless strategy is always part of God's plan and a requirement for His power to achieve ultimate glory and recognition.

In the case of Gideon's defeat of the Midianites, we will discern that God's seemingly doomed strategic maneuver was in fact part of a brilliant plan for the salvation of His people.

TRUST IN GOD

"And we know that in all things God works for the good of those who love Him."
— Romans 8:28

THE PRIMARY KEY TO VICTORY in spiritual warfare throughout the entire biblical narrative was absolute and complete reliance on the strength of God. The Psalmist wrote, "Some trust in chariots and some in horses but we trust in the name of the LORD our God."[13] However, although the Psalmist trusted God to bring their enemies to their knees and fall, it is important to further observe that spiritual warfare did not mean that a warrior could simply remain idle.

On all occasions of successful spiritual warfare, God required His people to take decisive action in a specific and oftentimes peculiar manner. Through strict obedience, faith, and reliance on the strength of God, victory was always claimed against overwhelming odds.

[13] Psalm 20:7

On the morning of Gideon's defeat of the Midianites, Gideon had gathered his 32,000 men in a military outpost near the spring of Harod. The enemy camp loomed in a nearby valley to the north of Gideon's perimeter. Anticipating a large-scale attack utilizing the collective strength of his vast army, Gideon was fully prepared for battle. However, God had other plans for Gideon that would ensure his success with only a small strike force of spiritually empowered warriors.

The LORD told Gideon, "You have too many men. I cannot deliver Midian into their hands, or Israel would boast against me and say, 'My own strength saved me.'"[14] Therefore, God commanded Gideon to announce to the army that anyone who trembled with fear would be permitted to depart the battlefield and not engage in the ensuing war. Hearing this announcement, 22,000 of Gideon's men picked up their weapons and left. However, God was still not satisfied, and devised a test to allow Gideon to discern those warriors who would ultimately secure victory. The LORD told Gideon to lead the remaining 10,000 men to a nearby stream to quench their thirst. Directing Gideon to carefully observe the specific way the men drank, God said, "Separate those who lap the water with their tongues as a dog laps from those who kneel down to drink."[15]

---

[14] Judges 7:2
[15] Judges 7:5

In the Book of Proverbs, it says, "Where there is no vision, the people perish."[16] Suddenly, through the unfolding biblical account of Gideon's assessment of the 10,000 soldiers, this verse comes alive with spiritually tactical relevance. We discover that 300 true warriors drank water from the stream with cupped hands; all the others kneeled down to drink, and in doing so lost situational awareness of their surroundings. In other words, by kneeling down at the water's edge, 9,700 soldiers "lost their vision" and were sent home.

With only 300 remaining warriors armed with just trumpets and jars containing torches, Gideon defeated the vastly greater numbered army of Midian. As Gideon and his men advanced on the enemy soldiers, their battle cry was, "For the LORD and for Gideon."[17] Hearing this battle cry, we discover the ultimate crushing blow came upon the Midianites not by the hand of Gideon's warriors, but by the very hand of God: "The LORD caused the men throughout the [Midian] camp to turn on each other with their swords."[18]

As we advance through the Bible in pursuit of faithfully understanding the full implications of spiritual warfare and the warrior archetype, let us pause to identify and review three critical elements thus far observed:

---

[16] Proverbs 29:18
[17] Judges 7:18
[18] Judges 7:22

1. God's selection of Gideon's 300 warriors was not random or arbitrary. God chose warriors who employed sound battlefield tactics and keen situational awareness. *God works best through those who are obedient and self-disciplined.*
2. Gideon and his warriors wholeheartedly knew their victory and strength was to be found in the LORD.[19] *God works best through those who rely on His strength.*
3. Success in Gideon's battle was not dependent upon advanced weapons or the overwhelming proportion of allied to enemy forces. *God works best through those who have bold faith in Him.*

---

[19] Judges 7:18 and 7:20 describe Gideon's warrior's battle cry as, "For the LORD."

SINGLE COMBAT

"I come against you in the name of the LORD Almighty."
— 1 Samuel 17:45

AS WE CONTINUE OUR JOURNEY of tracing the warrior archetype through the biblical narrative, we turn our attention from large-scale conflict to the arena of single combat. As the nature of the battlefield transitions from the entanglement of large armies to small and intimate clashes of will, we are presented with an excellent illustration for a greater understanding of spiritual warfare and the nuances of the biblical warrior.

In addition, the critical progression from macro-battle to micro-battle further demonstrates the way God utilized aspects of the warrior archetype to reveal Himself both within the narrative of the Bible and in our very soul. For the specific investigation of single combat, let us focus upon the battle of David and Goliath. This unique account within the Bible best represents the significant advancement of several key principles of immense importance for the modern-day spiritual warrior and follower of Christ.

The Book of Deuteronomy plants a towering stake in the ground for those who would confront injustice, evil, and discord in the world. "The LORD will grant that the enemies who rise up against you will be defeated before you."[20] David certainly understood this promise well because his bold advance upon Goliath would seem foolhardy at best, and absolute suicide at worst. However, building upon the principles established within large-scale spiritual warfare, we discover that David employed both a perfect combination of faith in God and decisively courageous action in the defeat of his opponent.

Let us begin by noting that David arrived on the battlefield as a shepherd boy bringing food to his brothers who were serving in King Saul's army.[21] In other words, David was not an enlisted soldier in the army. However, although not a soldier bearing arms and trained in military maneuver, David was a *warrior at heart*, and his faithful actions would ultimately win the day.[22] Arriving on scene just as the battle lines were being drawn, "David left his things with the keeper of supplies, ran to the battle lines, and asked his brothers how

---

[20] Deuteronomy 28:7
[21] Ref; 1 Samuel 17:15-19
[22] Ref; 1 Samuel 16:18

they were."[23] As David approached his brothers who were set near the front of the battle lines, Goliath stepped into view and shouted defiance at the Israelite army.

Although the army was "terrified and dismayed"[24] David stood his ground and asked, "What will be done for the man who kills this Philistine?"[25] This question provides insight into the mindset of David and encourages the cultivation of a key quality for the modern day spiritual warrior and follower of Jesus.

David employed perhaps the most important and vital weapon on the battlefield: the power of a positive mental attitude. Rather than fearing Goliath in the fashion of the Israelite army, David disciplined his mind to maintain optimism based on unequivocal faith in God. His question regarding the prize for the defeat of Goliath revealed that the battle had already been won in his mind. David knew that through a combination of his ultimate trust in God and mastery of the tools of his trade, he would surely succeed.

As the nature of spiritual warfare progressed from large-scale to single-combat the psychology of the battle advanced from the external to the internal realm. For example, as we further investigate the battle of David and Goliath, we observe the following:

---

[23] 1 Samuel 17:22
[24] 1 Samuel 17:11
[25] 1 Samuel 17:26

1. *Antagonists would attempt to elicit self-doubt in the warrior's mind.*
2. *Antagonists would challenge the warrior's destiny.*
3. *Antagonists would focus on the problem, not the solution.*

No sooner had David formulated his ultimate plan for the destruction of Goliath and put it into motion, then did David's own brother Eliab begin to ridicule and insult him: "With whom did you leave those few sheep in the wilderness?"[26] Note the subtle leverage of insult upon injury within this verse. First, Eliab reminded David that he was not a soldier, but merely a lonely shepherd boy. Adding fuel to the fire of insult, Eliab further ridiculed David for tending only to "a few sheep in the wilderness" rather than a large flock within a shepherd's grazing field.

Eliab was attempting to dissuade David from achieving his *destiny* as a true warrior for God by encouraging David to focus on his current *position* as a lowly shepherd. However, rather than surrendering to a negative mental attitude, David remained positive by aligning himself with God. Certain of his ability to succeed in battle, David requested that King Saul allow him to fight against Goliath.

---

[26] 1 Samuel 17:28

Building upon the principles of spiritual warfare employed in large-scale confrontation, we take note that David also utilized these same strategies with resounding success. When King Saul challenged David as to his ability to confront a trained warrior such as Goliath, David immediately replied that his success would come through God, not through his own strength. David had faced and defeated nature's most ferocious predatory animals including a lion and a bear. David was confident that the same God who "delivered him from the paw of the lion and the paw of the bear" would assure his victory from "the hand of this Philistine."[27]

David knew that his ability to defeat Goliath would be based on faith, and faith alone. King Saul's idea was to dress David up in his own armor, in effect making David as much like Goliath as possible. Finally relenting and giving David permission to face Goliath, it was on the condition that David wear the King's suit of armor and carry his sword into battle. David, however, renounced the entire principle because he knew that the victory was, "'Not by might, nor by power, but by my Spirit', saith the LORD of hosts."[28] Refusing to wear armor into battle and trusting solely in God and the tools of his shepherd's craft, David ran towards Goliath with the full assurance of God's Word on his tongue.

---

[27] 1 Samuel 17:37
[28] Zechariah 4:6

Emphasizing the wisdom and knowledge that God wins the victory when His children act decisively and with a full measure of faith, David exclaimed, "It is not by sword or spear that the LORD saves; for the battle is the LORD's."[29] Launching a rock from his sling, David struck Goliath squarely in the forehead. "The stone sank into his [Goliath's] forehead, and he fell facedown on the ground."[30] David had the anointing of God upon him and achieved the victory against Goliath because he had been faithful in the isolation and obscurity of countless nights alone in the shepherd's field.[31] His private testing in the wilderness allowed him to confidently stand in the public arena in the name of the Lord.

As we build our momentum in the investigation of spiritual warfare, it is imperative to reflect on a key principle of battlefield victory that God revealed through His Word. In all instances of spiritual warfare the definitive strategy of God was for His creation to maintain ultimate trust in Him. For this reason, we observe the way seemingly impossible odds of victory are achieved through the supernatural deliverance of God. Fewer soldiers overcome vast armies, and a single stone defeats a giant.

---

[29] 1 Samuel 17:47
[30] 1 Samuel 17:49
[31] Psalm 78:70-71

THE BATTLE FOR HEART AND MIND

"The LORD looks at the heart."
— 1 Samuel 16:7

AS WE PROGRESS OUR INVESTIGATION of spiritual warfare and the warrior archetype from the large-scale engagement to the intimate arena of single-combat, we finally arrive at the unifying battlefield waged within our individual heart and mind. We therefore conclude our study with the life and ministry of Jesus Christ, who continually admonished his apostles that the ultimate covenant relationship with God would be experienced and achieved by turning one's attention away from the world. Jesus explained this principle by warning against the temptation to search off in the distance for the presence of God. Jesus knew that the Kingdom of God was not some faraway destination, but was rather within the heart of every individual.

Therefore, Jesus intensified the battle by focusing not only upon human evil, but also on the cause of evil, which he identified as the "thief who comes to kill and destroy."[32] Only through the cultivation of a mind and heart like Jesus can we hope to defeat the "flaming arrows of the evil one"[33] and arrive before God as a victorious warrior, ready and willing to receive our inheritance with His exclamation: "Well done, my good and faithful servant."[34]

Our final arena of confrontation therefore takes place not on a field of battle so often associated with strife and struggle, yet rather within the "secret place"[35] of our very heart and mind. To investigate this secret place where the ultimate victory must be secured, we turn our attention to Jesus' decisive conquest over evil and the temptation of darkness. As the perfect example of a true spiritual warrior, we observe the type of confrontation Jesus faced, and even more importantly, how "what was intended to harm [him] God used for good."[36]

Following 40 days and nights of fasting and exposure to the wilderness, we discover that Jesus was hungry.[37] Sensing his opportunity for attack, Satan took aim at Jesus and loaded three high-powered and potentially lethal "fiery arrows"[38] into his quiver.

---

[32] John 10:10
[33] Ephesians 6;16
[34] Matthew 25:23
[35] Psalm 91:1
[36] Genesis 50:20
[37] Matthew 4:2
[38] Ephesians 6:16

The specific arrows were aimed at:

1. *God's provisions*
2. *God's promises*
3. *God's superiority*

For our investigative purposes, it is important to note the effect that physical hunger, exhaustion, and stress can have on the quality of our thinking. Although the modern-day spiritual warrior may never experience a true 40-day fasting from food, through the ebb and flow of the seasons of life, we may experience a fasting or lack of positivity and goodness within our mind. Knowing the potential weakness that hunger could invoke, "The tempter came to him and said, 'If you are the son of God, tell these stones to turn to bread.'"[39]

The first arrow was launched and hit from two directions. First, it challenged Jesus' divine identity as the Son of God. Second, because Jesus was both fully God and fully human, this attack challenged Jesus' basic human need for food and nourishment. Therefore, in our daily striving for "wisdom, stature and favor with God and man"[40] we must be prepared for attacks against our mind that would threaten our identity as "made in the image of God"[41] and our tendency to seek the material objects of the world for fulfillment.

---

[39] Matthew 4:3
[40] Luke 2:52
[41] Genesis 1:26

Anticipating the tempter's schemes, Jesus maneuvered out of the line of fire and then counterattacked with "the sword of the Spirit, which is the word of God."[42] Jesus replied with authority by quoting Old Testament scripture: "Man shall not live on bread alone, but on every word that comes from the mouth of God."[43] Rather than entertaining or wrestling with temptation, Jesus immediately invoked the power of God's Word. Therefore, employing the close-quarters tactic David utilized when he exclaimed, "The battle is the LORD's," we take special consideration that Jesus magnificently reinforced the significance of this same strategy.

By speaking the Word of God, Jesus provided an example and model for all spiritual warriors to follow. In every instance of opposition, temptation, and battlefield engagement, your key to victory will always be turning the reins over to God. This beautiful example of Jesus encourages the modern-day warrior to faithfully trust in God for every need, including both verbal encouragement and physical sustenance.

The second arrow was aimed directly at Jesus' confidence in the faithfulness of God. The tempter took Jesus to the Holy City and had him stand upon the highest point of the temple.

---

[42] Ephesians 6:17
[43] Matthew 4:4; cr., Deuteronomy 8:3

The tempter then said, “If you are the Son of God, throw yourself down. For it is written, ‘He will command his angels concerning you, and they will lift you up in their hands, so that you will not strike your foot against a stone,’” to which Jesus replied, “Do not put the LORD your God to the test.”[44]

In this attack, Jesus was pressured to face a very human fear: During seasons of challenge and in our moments of imperative need, will God come through? It is interesting to note the tempter once again chose to challenge and question Jesus’ identity as the Son of God. However, Jesus knew who he was and was confident that in times of trouble, opposition, and fiery attack, God would be his shield and sword. Jesus provided the perfect example for all spiritual warriors: The key to victory will always be absolute dependence on God.

The third and final arrow was aimed at Jesus’ certainty in the absolute superiority of God. The temptation many of us face on a regular and consistent basis is the illusion of self-sufficiency rather than in God’s ability “to supply all our needs.”[45] Therefore, we observe the tempter’s proposed shortcut to dependence upon God: “If you worship me, it will be yours.”[46] For our purposes, it is important to note

---

[44] Matthew 4:5-7
[45] Philippians 4:19

the "worship" in question may not necessarily be outright worship of the tempter, but rather the "little foxes which spoil the vine."[47] Independence, self-righteousness, envy, fear, and greed are the enemy forces that limit our ability to access the sovereign power of God.

To simultaneously defend and counter-attack the final onslaught against his mind and heart, Jesus once again called upon the mighty authority of God's Word: "You must worship the LORD your God and serve only Him."[48] In this manner, Jesus professed an absolutely critical truth for the modern day spiritual warrior. Regardless of the strength of our physical assets (*the outward appearance*) our ultimate strength will be found in God and our identity in Jesus Christ (*the heart*).[49]

---

[46] Matthew 4:9

[47] Song of Solomon 2:15

[48] Matthew 4:10

[49] Colossians 2:10. The temptation to trust in our own wisdom, strength, or the "idols of our heart" is of grave danger for the follower of Christ. The first biblical evidence of this was witnessed in the anointing of King David when the LORD told the prophet Samuel: "Although people look at the outward appearance, the LORD looks at the heart" (1 Samuel 16:7). For review of this critical principle, refer to the introductory section of this book.

SPIRITUAL TOOLS AND TACTICS FOR THE WARRIOR

"Put on the full armor of God."
— Ephesians 6:11

AS WE ADVANCE THROUGH the Bible in pursuit of a faithful understanding of a true spiritual warrior, we are now in a superior position to assess our terrain and reach several conclusions. We begin by noting that as children made in the image of God we each have unique "Heavenly gifts" that bear resemblance to our Creator, the most universal of which is the archetype of the warrior. Throughout the Bible, God continually revealed Himself as a warrior.[50] Therefore, by invoking the Word of God and His presence in our life, we can "push back our adversaries; His name will trample down those who rise against us."[51]

[50] Ref; Exodus 15:3
[51] Psalm 44:5

Regardless of our individually chosen profession or career field, within our very heart and mind resides the archetype of a warrior, instilled within us by God when we were still "in our mother's womb."[52] Therefore, embracing your identity as a spiritual warrior is often the first step to ensuring victory in any area of your life. As a spiritual warrior annointed by God, your mindset should be one of eagerness to be deployed onto the ultimate battlefield of life.

Our investigation of spiritual warfare throughout the biblical account provides us wisdom to understand that battlefield victory has less to do with external realities, and more to do with the "secret place" of our heart and mind. For this reason, a bold new interpretation of the true spiritual warrior is presented before us as follows:

[52] Jeremiah 1:5

WARRIOR

W = Win first in the mind.
"Our God gives us a spirit of power, love and self-discipline." — 2 Timothy 1:7

A = Affirm God as your true source of strength.
"I can do all things through Christ who strengthens me." — Philippians 4:13

R = Run towards the challenge.
"And let us run with endurance the race set out before us." — Hebrews 12:1

R = Remain positive and prepared for battle.
"Stand firm, with the belt of truth buckled around your waist." — Ephesians 6:14

I = Inhale the presence of God.
"The breath of the Almighty gives me life." — Job 33:4

O = Orient your thinking and speaking to align with God's Word.
"The sword of the spirit is the Word of God." — Ephesians 6:17

R = Remain faithful to the promise of God's Word.
"The LORD preserves the faithful." — Psalm 31:23

Throughout the entire biblical narrative, spiritual warfare and the warrior archetype are themes of resounding importance. In order to faithfully abide within the new covenant established through the life and ministry of Jesus, embracing the archetype of the spiritual warrior is absolutely critical to ensure battlefield success and the accomplishment of your purpose in life. Through the warrior mindset and donning of "the full armor of God"[53] you can faithfully resist the fiery attacks of evil and temptation. In the same manner that Jesus courageously "closed with and destroyed the enemy"[54] you can trust God during every season to provide victory in the temporal life you now enjoy and the eternal life that is still to come.

---

[53] Ephesians 6:14-17

[54] Hebrews 2:14b. Reference creed of the U.S. Army Solider

PART TWO

FINISHING THE RACE

STAYING THE COURSE

"They charge like warriors, they scale walls like soldiers. They run and do not swerve from their course."

— Joel 2:7

"Let us fix our eyes on Jesus."

— Hebrews 12:2

FINISHING A RACE, whether in sport or in life, implies being able to see the finish line. However, oftentimes the finish line of the race we are engaged in is so far in the distance, and the terrain that we race upon is so treacherous, that we are compelled to simply take one step at a time.

Early in my military career, a longtime mentor of mine pulled me aside and said, "Greg, good leaders are able to reveal things to subordinates they could otherwise never see on their own." His words resonated deep within my soul and I was held captive by the idea that something obvious to me could be seemingly invisible to someone else. The implications on the battlefield were immense: Unless I opened the eyes of my soldiers and helped them see potential dangers within their midst, catastrophic injury would surely be their end. However, once the danger was revealed to them, their "battlefield knowledge" would increase and they would be more likely to navigate risk independent of my supervision. And perhaps even more encouraging, with their newfound wisdom the subordinate soldier would be in a position to help reveal to their peers what they would never see on their own.

In many respects and to a varying degree, we are all soldiers and long-distance runners on the battlefield of life. Twists, turns, peaks, and valleys are part of the terrain we need to successfully navigate in order to reach our final destination. However, in addition to dangerous valleys, there are also magnificent mountaintops that our soul longs to summit. Yet, unless revealed to us by a trusted source of wisdom and knowledge much greater than our own, the tendency is to rely on our independent understanding, which often leads to a closed loop of crisscrossing back and forth across the dark valleys of life.[55]

---

[55] Ref; Proverbs 3:5-6

REVELATION OF GOD

"I pray that the God of our Lord Jesus Christ, the Father of glory, might give you the spirit of wisdom and revelation in the knowledge of Him."

— Ephesians 1:17

I RECALL LEARNING THE FUNDAMENTALS of land navigation during U.S. Army Basic Officer Leadership Training in the hills of North Dakota. During daylight hours the task was fairly simple. Given a compass and map, I navigated across open terrain to specific points or "plots" that my instructor had assigned me. However, in the pitch-black night, not being able to see the tips of my fingers on my outstretched arm, the task became altogether impossible.

One night, that was very characteristic of North Dakota summers, there was a great lightning storm. Although startling and a bit nerve-wracking, I soon discovered the lightning was a blessing in disguise. When the lightning struck, the terrain all around me was instantly illuminated, much like a flare bursting in the night. For a few seconds the imprint of my surroundings made an impression on my mind. I could essentially "see in the dark." Although brief, those momentary intervals of revelation of my surroundings were enough to allow me to successfully complete the navigation course.

In the Book of Proverbs it says: "Where there is no vision, the people perish."[56] In order to navigate the battlefield of life we need to clearly identify the obstacles before us. However, as my mentor counseled me years ago, we also need a trusted source to reveal to us what we could otherwise not see on our own. This idea of "not being able to see on our own" is further expressed in Proverbs: "Be not wise in thy own eyes."[57] In other words, if we rely on our own understanding, knowledge, and worldly acquired wisdom, we will not be able to see clearly.

The potential pitfall and shortcoming of limited understanding and "battlefield blindness" was certainly at the heart of the Apostle Paul in his letter to the Ephesians. In Ephesians 1:17 we read, "I pray that the God of our Lord Jesus Christ, the Father of glory, might give you the spirit of wisdom and revelation in the knowledge of Him." Expressed another way, Paul's prayer was that God would grant us a specific type of spiritual wisdom we could otherwise never arrive at on our own.

---

[56] Proverbs 29:18
[57] Proverbs 3:7

We may interpret through verse 17 that Paul was specifically describing a type of wisdom that could only be achieved through the power and working of the Holy Spirit. Paul specifically prayed the Ephesians would experience a supernatural endowment of wisdom that was only possible through God's revelation of Himself. Paul's contention therefore was to ensure the believer understood that worldly wisdom, gained through the intellect of humanity, would never be enough to truly know the "surpassing greatness"[58] of God. Paul's use of the term "revelation" referred to God's own self-disclosure, which would be experienced supernaturally by the believer.

In the New Testament Epistle of James, the author made clear the distinction between wisdom of the world and wisdom revealed by God. James describes worldly wisdom as "earthly, unspiritual and demonic."[59] In the context of navigating the battlefield of life, the result of following and "seeing" through the eyes of our own wisdom is like a landmine waiting to be stepped upon. A torrential explosion of "envy, selfish ambition, disorder and evil"[60] is dangerously underfoot.

---

[58] Ephesians 1:19
[59] James 3:15-16
[60] James 3:15-16

The Apostle Paul foresaw the treacherous terrain the Ephesians, in addition to future believers, would need to safely transverse. Through his prayer, Paul's hope was that God would reveal Himself to us. Through this supernatural revelation, our wisdom and knowledge would be increased to heavenly proportion, which is distinctly different and abundantly more important than worldly wisdom.

James articulated this difference in verse 3:17: "Wisdom that comes from heaven is first of all pure, then peace-loving, considerate, submissive, full of mercy and good fruit, impartial and sincere." With this newfound perspective of "Heavenly wisdom" held in mind, we turn once again to the beauty and magnitude of the opening line of Paul's prayer. With gratitude in our heart, we discover that Paul prayed that you and I would have a direct experience of the power and glory of God. Like a flash of lightning in the middle of a dark night, Paul's prayer was such that you would experience an imprint of God in your mind and heart, and that through His divine revelation your spiritual wisdom would be increased.

THE EYES OF THE HEART

"I pray that the eyes of your heart would be enlightened."

— Ephesians 1:18

THE SECOND COMPONENT OF PAUL'S PRAYER for the Ephesians was equally inspiring and complemented the revelation of God invoked in verse 17. Paul prayed, "Since the eyes of your heart have been enlightened, that you would know what is the hope of His calling, what are the riches of the glory of His inheritance in the saints."[61] By focusing on Paul's use of the word "heart" in this verse, and through an understanding of the bodily function of the heart, we can truly appreciate the magnitude of Paul's prayer.

Being made in the image of God,[62] we have an ordained birthright and divine capacity to know and *experience* the presence of God. Before going any further, let us turn our attention to the words of Jesus who said, "This is eternal life, *that they may know you*, the one true God, and Jesus Christ,

---

[61] Ephesians 1:18
[62] Genesis 1:27

whom you have sent."[63] Oftentimes, when reading the Bible and the words of Jesus it is equally important to note what Jesus said in addition to what Jesus *did not say*. Therefore, take special consideration that Jesus' prayer was for you and I to *know God*. He did not say, "Know *about* God." In other words, Jesus' prayer and hope was that you would have a direct experience and firsthand knowledge of God. And now, through the words of Paul in Ephesians verse 1:17, we arrive at the understanding that this knowledge of God will not be possible through our own understanding or human intellect. Knowing God is a supernatural experience, which is the direct result of God revealing Himself to us in His Word and through His Son.

In the context of a personal relationship, this makes total and complete sense. No matter how hard we might try, in order to really know someone they ultimately need to reveal their mind and soul to us. This specific type of "revelation," understood through verse 18 of Paul's prayer, was experienced within the "eyes of our heart," which were enlightened through the revelation of God. In the same way our mind has thinking, reasoning, and intellectual capacities, Paul understood our heart shared these capacities on an even deeper and more spiritually significant level. In fact, according to Paul, the mind may have even blunted the true spiritual wisdom of the heart.

---

[63] John 17:3 – Use of italics are the authors emphasis.

In Corinthians, Paul wrote, "Their minds are made dull because a veil covers their hearts."[64] We can interpret through Ephesians 1:17-18 that Paul's prayer for the believer was to "see" that if truth, wisdom, and knowledge about God was to be faithfully grasped, then the heart must be enlightened. Furthermore, as the heart is a central and life-sustaining organ of the body, it is responsible for moving both blood and oxygen throughout the entire circulatory system. Thus, when Paul prays for the "eyes of our heart to be enlightened" he is praying that in addition to knowing *about* God at the intellectual level of our mind, that through the circulation of God's love throughout every cell of our body, we would be "enlightened" to truly *know* God by the revelation of His presence.

Finally, it is important to note that in the Bible, the word "heart" often referred to the genuine self as distinguished from appearance, identification with the mind, and physical presence.[65] And this "heart-self" had its own nature, character, and disposition, which ultimately affected the thoughts, words, and actions of the believer.[66] Therefore, a believer whose "heart" was illuminated by the revelation of God would radically change the entire makeup of their life and would never be the same again.

---

[64] 2 Corinthians 3:14-15

[65] Walter A. Elwell and Barry J. Beitzel, "Wisdom, Wisdom Literature," *Baker Encyclopedia of the Bible* (Grand Rapids, MI: Baker Book House, 1988), p. 2149.

[66] Ibid; p. 2149.

Due to the tendency of our human intellect to attach through the senses to material objects and "desires of the flesh,"[67] Paul's prayer centered on *spiritual* acquisition. For example, we observed that in verse 17, Paul's hope was that we would acquire *spiritual wisdom* in the knowledge of God. Through the revelation of God in our lives, the eyes of our heart would be enlightened, allowing us to faithfully see what truly mattered most. Therefore, as we continue to journey though the totality of Paul's prayer, we observe the "riches" that Paul is desirous of us seeing and inheriting are meant to be enjoyed spiritually and not worldly.

We take note that verse 18 concluded with Paul's use of the word, "inheritance." This word is of immense importance, and is best understood through the context of the Old Testament. Time and time again, God referred to His creation as His own inheritance. In Deuteronomy, we read that God took His creation "as the people of His inheritance"[68] and that God's people were "his own inheritance, redeemed by His great power."[69] As sons and daughters of God, our relationship with Him is similar to that of Father and child.

The intimacy of this relationship is absolutely vital for us to comprehend and was at the heart of Jesus' ministry. In the first two words of the "Lord's Prayer" Jesus explained the

---

[67] Galatians 5:17
[68] Deuteronomy 4:20
[69] Deuteronomy 9:26

nature of our relationship with God by the declaration: “Our Father.”[70] In this manner, Jesus invoked our understanding of the divine connection to our “Father of glory.”[71] Jesus embraced and perfectly articulated the magnitude of this relationship and his divine right to the inheritance of his Father when he declared, “All I have is yours, and all you have is mine.”[72]

Paul’s prayer as expressed in verse 18 is therefore twofold. First, his hope is that we would embrace our relationship with God as that of Father and child. Secondly, through the context of this Fatherly relationship and through spiritual revelation, Paul prayed that we would receive our true inheritance as sons and daughters of God. It is exceedingly important to take note of Paul’s use of the word “glory,” which is evident in both verse 17 and 18. In verse 17 God was declared to be the “Father of glory.” Throughout the Old Testament the glory of God was oftentimes so bright and of such overwhelming power that it was shrouded in a cloud.[73] However, in verse 18 we discover the brilliance and intensity of God’s glory is to be shared with us as a component of our inheritance as children of God.

---

[70] Matthew 6:9
[71] Ephesians 1:17
[72] John 17:10
[73] Exodus 16:10

GOD'S SURPASSING GREATNESS

"And his incomparably great power for us who believe."
— Ephesians 1:19

FINALLY, IN VERSE 19 OF PAUL'S PRAYER, we take special note of the connection between the "surpassing greatness" and power of God in direct proportion toward those who believe in Him: "And what is the surpassing greatness of His power towards us who believe, in accordance with the working of the strength of His might."[74] As described by Paul, it was according to one's level of belief, which was furthermore achieved only through God's revelation of Himself, that a believer could fully experience the "strength of His might."

Paul's use of the phrase "surpassing greatness," when understood within the context of navigating the battlefield of life, is worthy of our thankfulness and delight. "Surpassing" can best be understood as "superior" or ranking higher than any other type of power, regardless of how immense our

---

[74] Ephesians 1:19

intellect may attempt to convince us it is. The magnificent, supreme, and nearly incomprehensible power of God's greatness is directed with love towards those who believe in Him. Through God's own revelation of Himself we may thus be faithfully "inherited" into His enduring love and embrace.

Navigating the battlefield of life can be a treacherous task, full of unsuspecting danger. However, this same battlefield when faithfully illuminated, can become a place of beauty and spiritual splendor. In order for the terrain around us to become visible, a transformation will need to take place within both our mind and heart. The biblical word "Grace" was described to me once as the "effect of God giving us what we do not deserve," and "Mercy" taking place when "God *does not give us* what we do deserve." Paul's prayer invokes this very measure of grace; his hope is that you and I would experience the revelation of God, and through this supernatural opening and enlightenment of the "eyes of our heart" we would fully embrace our right to an inheritance of epic proportion.

PART THREE

KEEPING THE FAITH

LEADERSHIP BEGINS WITH YOU

"Remember your leaders and immitate their way of life."
— Hebrews 13:7

KEEPING THE FAITH REQUIRES that you lead yourself first and set a positive example for others to follow.

Leadership in military and public safety professions is often referred to as "the warrior's art" that is ultimately responsible for mission success, esprit de corps, and unit cohesiveness.[75] Effective leadership frequently results in a unified feeling of pride, enthusiastic fellowship, and common loyalty shared by members of a particular group.[76] I firmly believe that the exposition of biblical leadership has immense and relevant implications for leaders within the military and public safety sector, as well as for anyone who feels compelled to lead in their respective field of influence.

One of the biggest misunderstandings people have about leadership is that they think it is based on position or rank. However, this is not necessarily the case. Although oftentimes the

---

[75] Christopher Kolenda. *Leadership: The Warriors Art.* (Army War College Foundation Press, June 1, 2001), p. 54.
[76] Ibid.

appointed rank or position is consistent with the ability of the leader, many times it is not. As one of my mentors explained to me years ago: "It's not the rank that makes the leader. The leader makes the rank." Subordinates may be compelled and legally required to obey the commands of a leader's rank or position. However, a true leader is able to inspire followership and motivate excellence with everyone around them independent of their rank, title, or position.

The key to biblical leadership is to remember *you are leading people to Christ.* In addition, the real secret to the power and influence of the biblically focused leader is their ability to humble themselves to the greatest leader of all—our Lord Jesus Christ.

The Bible is rich with wonderful examples of leadership. One of my favorites is the account of the faith and leadership responsibility of Abraham. I believe that this particular account is important for it reveals a key leadership theme that subsequently runs throughout the entire Bible.

Scripture reveals that one day God delivered a message to Abraham that would radically change the remainder of his life—and the life of all humanity. The Lord said to Abraham, "Leave your country, your people and your father's household and go to the land I will show you."[77] Imagine the shock, fear, and anxiety that Abraham must have felt in that moment. Abraham had been

---

[77] Genesis 12:1

told to leave everything behind: his family, his way of life, his possessions, and most importantly, *his way of thinking.* To complicate matters, God did not tell Abraham exactly where he was going or what he would do when he got there. God seemed to challenge Abraham to "take a step of faith" and to just start moving in a general direction. God would not let Abraham know *where he was going* until he had the courage to *just get going!*

This was Abraham's first leadership test, and in many respects, this is the test of all biblically minded leaders: Will you believe in God and trust Him to lead you into an *uncertain future*? Or, will you remain where you are comfortable, and hang onto a *certain present and past*?

Abraham trusted God and went, and in the process provided an inspiring example for you to follow. The book of Hebrews summarizes what happened next: "By faith Abraham, when called to go to a place he would later receive as his inheritance, obeyed and went, even though he did not know where he was going."[78]

By faith.

Abraham obeyed God and went.

Even though Abraham did not know exactly where he was going.

---

[78] Hebrews 11:8

I believe this is the model of leadership that God wants you to embrace. Many people never realize their potential and fulfill their purpose in life because they lack the faith to trust God to lead them into the great unknown. Sadly, many times the promise of what the Bible refers to as "*your inheritance*" is less promising than the "*comfortable paneled house that you currently live in.*"[79]

Biblically minded leaders trust God to take the reins of their life. Continuing the lesson of Abraham, when you put God first and trust in His leadership, God will fulfill the following promises in your life:

I will make you into a great nation

And I will bless you;

I will make your name great,

And you will be a blessing.

I will bless those who bless you,

And curse those who curse you;

And all peoples on earth will be blessed through you.[80]

---

[79] Haggai 1:4
[80] Genesis 12:2-3

Consider the awesome implications that these promises from God have in store for your life. The reference to "great nation" means the manifestation of your dreams, goals, and aspirations. In the Bible, someone's "name" refers to his or her essence, character, and essential qualities. When the God of the Universe *blesses your name and makes it great*, He increases the good qualities of your nature that inherently result in your ability to lead yourself and others. When *God blesses your name*, He removes obstacles from your path, while simultaneously organizing a series of time-space events and divine appointments that result in doors of opportunity opening right before your very eyes.

THE TRUE COST OF LEADERSHIP

"Even though I walk through the darkest valley."
— Psalm 23:4

BIBLICAL LEADERSHIP IS NOT FOR THE FAINT OF HEART, and there is often a hefty price to pay. If you would aspire to the position of a leader capable of inspiring voluntary followership, then you must recognize that there is a perpetual reckoning of self-discipline that you must be prepared to make. Sometimes it is the price of loneliness; sometimes it is being misunderstood, endless days of testing, of having few friends, or of being ridiculed for devotion to a higher ideal. It could be an assortment of things, but one thing will always remain certain: There is a high price to pay for keeping your life right before God.

It is only a matter of time for the person who makes the decision to follow God to discover that for a season they are walking alone. This temporal period of obscurity is part of God's plan to refine, strengthen, and prepare you to lead His flock. After David was anointed to be Israel's next King, he returned to the solitude of the shepherd's field in order to further develop the faith in God that would enable his victory over Goliath.

Very often, God prepares you to achieve the fullness of your destiny *by who and what He removes from your life*, rather than *by who and what He ushers in.* If your intention is the biblical model of leadership, then everything that stands in opposition to God must be condemned and cast aside. Similarly, everything in your life that can be used to glorify God must come entirely under His ownership and command. Before God will use your life to lead and bless others, He will first require a demonstration of your capacity and commitment to follow and glorify Him.[(i)]

If you want to lead yourself and others in an awesome way, the first step will always be putting God first in your life. When you put your faith in God and trust Him to lead you, then God will position you to lead others.

LEAD YOURSELF FIRST

"Commit your way to the LORD."
— Psalm 37:5

FROM MY WALK WITH GOD, I have learned that in order to be an authentic and credible leader, you must achieve self-mastery in service of others. In other words, you must lead yourself first. Therefore, even should you find yourself isolated on a remote island, you would nevertheless retain a vital and coveted leadership role: *You* would be responsible for *leading you.* The principle involved and progressive hierarchy of self-mastery and self-leadership that is evident within the Bible is best understood through a simple equation:

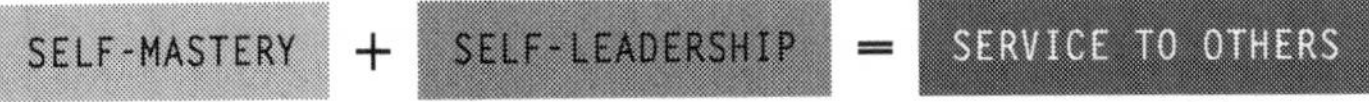

Self-mastery for the purpose of self-leadership with the intention of service to others is the supreme model of biblical leadership. Furthermore, while effective leadership on the battlefield, on the street, and in the boardroom is held responsible for mission success, preservation of life, and business prosperity, biblical leadership is supremely responsible for Kingdom success and perseveration of the soul.[81]

In the study of biblical leadership two essential principles immediately present themselves as worthy of examination and close consideration:

1. Leadership is the art of inspiring the act of *voluntary followership.*
2. Leadership is the art of setting a *positive example* for others to follow.

Effective leadership should inspire *voluntary* followership. The individual or group must *desire* to be guided, influenced, directed, and motivated by the person who wants to be considered the leader. Voluntary leadership is beautifully illustrated in the account of Jesus calling his disciples: "Going on from there, Jesus saw two other brothers, James son of Zebedee and his brother John. Jesus called them, and *immediately they left the boat and their father and followed him.*"[82]

---

[81] In Matthew 10:28, Jesus said, "Do not be afraid of those who kill the body but cannot kill the soul. Rather, be afraid of the One who can destroy both soul and body in hell." This particular scripture encapsulates the exceedingly important role of leaders, and definitively illustrates the difference between worldly and biblical leadership. The biblical leader must always remember that God will determine the fruits of their influence.

[82] Matthew 4:21-22. Author's use of italics to emphasize the voluntary aspect of the two brothers' eagerness to follow Jesus.

In addition to inspiring voluntary followership, an effective leader must set a *positive example* for others to follow. Setting a positive example establishes a leader independent of rank, appointment, or assignment. For example, in the account of David's leadership before he was appointed King, it is important to note: "All the tribes of Israel came to David at Hebron and said, 'We are your own flesh and blood. In the past, while Saul was king over us, *you were the one who led* Israel on their military campaigns.'"[83] This verse encourages leaders to understand that their actions are the determining factor in inspiring followership. Even before he became King, the tribes of Israel were inspired by David's leadership and were eager to voluntarily follow him.

Proper modeling and acute awareness of the positive aspects of biblical leadership are just as important as knowledge of the devastating consequences of failing to heed the Bible's advice. Although some leaders by position or rank can simply demand that others do as they are told, this type of leader does not inspire voluntary followership. Problems of coercion run rampant in a reward and punishment-based leadership model and only tend to elicit forced followership.

---

[83] 2 Samuel 5:2. Author's use of italics.

Furthermore, appointed leaders who *push from the rear* as opposed to the biblical model of *leading from the front* set an example with their actions that oftentimes contradicts their verbal orders. Considering the implications of leadership from the perspective of the follower, the only logical model of leadership one would enthusiastically and voluntary choose to follow would be based upon leadership by positive example.

By establishing congruency with your thoughts, words, and actions, you can achieve the capacity to faithfully lead others by inspiring a spirit of voluntary followership in any endeavor or environment.

As demonstrated in the life of King David and the perfect example of Jesus Christ, a leader need not wait until the assignment of rank or position in order to positively influence other people. Trust in the sequencing of God's divine design if you would aspire to lead others:

1. *Trust and follow God with all your heart.*
2. *Endure seasons of testing and obscurity.*
3. *Lead yourself first and achieve self-mastery in the service of others.*
4. *Defeat every Goliath of self-doubt and fear.*
5. *Authentically and credibly proclaim, "Come, and follow me!"*

LEADING THE WAY

"Go and make disciples of all nations."
— Matthew 28:19

DISCIPLE-MAKING AND LEADERSHIP ARE two sides of the same coin. If you are to take seriously the Word of God and the commands of our Lord Jesus Christ, then you must at once go about the task of *leading others* and *making disciples*. In many respects, the very purpose and existence of the Church can be found within these words from Jesus: "Therefore go [lead others] and *make disciples* of all nations, baptizing them in the name of the Father and of the Son and of the Holy Spirit, and teaching them to obey everything I have commanded you."[84]

At the center of the biblical methodology on leadership is the observance of a single-purposed mission: Jesus is calling you to make him the *unum neccessarum* (the one thing necessary) of your entire life.[85] Although in the secular world priorities are often perceived to exist on a graduated

---

[84] Matthew 28:19-20. My use of italics and exegesis within the brackets to emphasize Jesus' command for both *leading others* and *disciple-making*.
[85] Matthew 6:33.

scale from least to most important, Jesus is commanding something altogether different. "Jesus is calling his disciples to make him and his way of life, including the rights and wrongs of his design, *the priority of your life*."[86]

In love and obedience to Jesus, you must release the grasp of the "desires of the flesh"[87] and leave behind your old ways of thinking and behaving in exchange for a new identity in Christ.[88] By following Jesus, you begin to participate in the divinely anointed activity of increasing in his likeness and image.[89] In other words, through the power of God working within the deepest recesses of your heart, you begin the process of becoming like the Master himself.[90] Although continuing to purposely and productively engage within the world, you begin to reflect and image a union with God that permeates every area of your life.[91] Soon enough you will authentically and credibly begin to disciple and lead others, even as you continue to follow Christ.[92]

---

86 Rick Taylor. *The Anatomy of a Disciple*. (Well Community Church, Columbia, SC, 2013), p. 137.
87 Galatians 5:19-21
88 2 Corinthians 5:17
89 Ref. Romans 8:28-30 and 2 Corinthians 3:18.
90 Michael Wilkins. *Following The Master*. (Zondervan Publishing, Grand Rapids, MI: 1992), p. 41.
91 Taylor, p. 17.
92 1 Corinthians 11:1

Quite apart from the secular models of leading, coaching, consulting, and even counseling, which tend to compartmentalize and isolate parts of the human experience, the path of biblical leadership involves inviting Jesus into every area of one's life. Nothing is hidden. No stone can be left unturned. Our Lord's goal for his first group of leaders was that his life and teaching would be embodied within them and demonstrated to others. Jesus taught that "the best way to show people how to love others, is for them to be loved by you."[93] This spiritual formula for leadership would then be subsequently and perpetually reproduced until Christ's triumphant return.

Thus we see both the implications and implicitness of Jesus' method: Before discipling and leading others, the leader must first be trained. If a leader was first adequately trained and a level of self-mastery achieved, then they would be in an advantageous position to reproduce lives that would be like their own.[94] The second step for the leader was to "go and make disciples."[95]

---

[93] Dr. Bill Clem. Western Seminary Discipleship lecture. November, 2019.
[94] Robert Coleman. *The Master Plan of Evangelism*. (Revell Books, Grand Rapids, MI: 1993), p. 161.
[95] Matthew 28:19

In the disciple-making process, leaders invite people into God's story and equip them to share it with others.[96] In other words, it was not for the purpose of increasing Church attendance, developing new programs, or creating cleverly orchestrated worship ceremonies to which Jesus commissioned his first leaders. Rather, it was developing leaders who could in turn build other leaders.[97]

---

[96] Clem. November, 2019.
[97] Coleman, pp. 96-97.

THE LANDSCAPE OF LEADERSHIP

"Behold, I am sending you out like sheep among wolves."
— Matthew 10:16

A SURVEY OF THE PROBLEMS AND CHALLENGES facing modern society are staggering. It reveals increasing divorce rates, abandoned children, a billion dollar pornography industry, metal detectors in schools, senseless acts of rampage shootings, the normalization of sin on television, and a decline in Church attendance juxtaposed with an increasing number of Church leaders becoming involved in scandals normally reserved for politicians on Wall Street.[98] Even worse is the vast number of children and youth who are searching for identity that is readily available in religious institutions and places of worship; they are instead finding solace and meaning in drugs, alcohol, television, social media, on-line gaming, and criminal gangs.[99]

---

98 Patrick Morley. *How God Makes Men.* (Multnomah Books, New York, N: 2013), p. 137.
99 Federal report on youth and gangs at Youth.Gov (youth.gov/youth-topics/pregenting-gang-involvement/federal-data).

However, perhaps the most alarming and revealing indication of how difficult the times are is the overwhelming number of police suicides our nation experiences each year.[100] For the third straight year in row, the number of reported police suicides is three times higher than the number of officers killed in violent encounters with criminal offenders.[101] When those sworn to protect and serve our nation's heartland are the very same ones so overwhelmed by the problems they face that suicide becomes the answer, then indeed society has their back up against a seemingly insurmountable wall.

The biblical solution to these problems is leadership. When Jesus told his disciples to *lead others* and *make disciples*, he intended to release the power of his gospel on every problem we would ever encounter. In many respects, the Bible frames leadership and disciple-making as a moral issue.[102] In other words, leadership is a choice between right and wrong—a crossroads between obedience and disobedience.

---

[100] Huffington Post national criminal report on police suicide. January 2, 2019.
[101] BlueHelp.org
[102] Morley, p. 137.

When Jesus said, "If you love me, obey my commands,"[103] his implied expectation for leadership and disciple-making was either being part of the solution, or part of the problem.

The battle lines are drawn. Biblical leaders must take an active part in *calling*, *equipping,* and *sending* good soldiers of Jesus Christ to the front lines of spiritual warfare.[104] This is achieved through a program of biblical leaders who go out and make disciples. Our great commission is commanded by Jesus and witnessed throughout the Bible:

- "You will receive power when the Holy Spirit comes on you, and you will be my witness."[105]
- "Teach these truths to other trustworthy people who will be able to pass them on to others."[106]
- "As the Father has sent me, I am sending you."[107]
- "In everything set an example by doing good."[108]
- "A student is not above his teacher, but everyone who is fully trained will be like their teacher."[109]
- "Be *imitators* of us and of the Lord; become a *model* for all believers."[110]

---

[103] John 14:15
[104] 2 Timothy 2:3
[105] Acts 1:8
[106] 2 Timothy 2:2 (New Living Translation).
[107] John 20:21
[108] Titus 2:7
[109] Luke 6:40
[110] 1 Thessalonians 1:6-7. My use of italics and paraphrasing within this Scripture.

The moral implications of these verses are implicit. Believing that Jesus is the Son of God who died for our sins will ensure salvation.[111] However, it will not satisfy the requirement of having a plan to lead and disciple every willing person that we encounter. Jesus *called* his first disciples so that he could *teach* them how to walk with him in the world.[112] In other words, the initial *calling* led to *teaching* that resulted in *equipping* for the purpose of *sending* to *lead* others. When the disciples were with Jesus, class was always in session. Everything that Jesus said and did was a lesson, and since the disciples were almost always with Jesus, they were absorbing his teaching practically every moment that they were by his side.[113]

The blueprint of leadership that Jesus developed did not simply end with *learning lessons from the Master*. It involved both theory and application.[114] Learning and doing.[115] Absorbing and demonstrating.[116] Coming and going.[117] Jesus' expectation was that a leader would go and make disciples. Our method of discipleship and leadership should therefore be the same.

---

[111] Romans 10:9
[112] Wilkins, p. 22.
[113] Coleman. p. 68.
[114] Acts 5:12
[115] Luke 9:1-2
[116] Acts 2:1-4
[117] Luke 10:1

THE HEART OF THE MATTER

"Above all else, guard your heart."
— Proverbs 4:23

A LEADER HAS A HEART FOR GOD. In the Bible, the use of the word *heart* often refers to the innermost nature of the individual—the very seat of the human beings deepest and strongest emotions and desires.[118] A biblical leader has a heart that hungers and thirsts for a life with Jesus. In other words, God must see Himself within the heart of a leader.[119] Unlike secular leadership, mentorship, and self-mastery programs that offer a definitive course of study and anticipated day of graduation, the path of biblical leadership is a full immersion commitment for the totality of one's life on earth. Furthermore, in the process of becoming more like Jesus, each individual leader is increasingly equipped and commissioned for the responsibility of leading others.[120]

---

[118] Walter A. Elwell and Barry J. Beitzel. "Wisdom, Wisdom Literature" in *Baker Encyclopedia of the Bible* (Grand Rapids, MI: Baker House, 1998), p. 2149.
[119] Clem. November, 2019.
[120] Wilkins, p. 42.

Jesus taught that the first and greatest commandment was to love God with all your heart, soul, and mind, and the second was to love your neighbor as yourself.[121] When you reflect on the fact that you are made in the image of God, the fundamental principle that Jesus was teaching becomes clear. Because God relates to His creation as a loving Father, and you are made in His image, as image bearers of God you should therefore love God and other people. In this sense, as you grow in the likeness of Jesus, you will begin to increasingly reflect and demonstrate Jesus' attributes, character, and way of life to others.[122] At the most fundamental level, leaders love God and others as God loves them.

And here we see the greatest enemy and threat to biblical leadership: Most of us are not yet filled with the Truth of God's love.[123] If we were made to reflect God and to be His image bearers, what went wrong? In Genesis we find our answer. Rather than loving God, Adam and Eve turned their love from God onto themselves. In other words, instead of loving God as Jesus commanded, they "became lovers of pleasure rather than lovers of God."[124] Eve noticed the tree on the fruit was *pleasing* to look at and *desirable* for

---

[121] Matthew 22:36-29
[122] Acts 4:13
[123] Reference Romans 3:23 and Psalm 5:9
[124] 2 Timothy 3:4

gaining wisdom for *herself*.[125] In this sense, the love that Eve should have focused on God became twisted, perverted, and misdirected—it was focused only on herself.[126]

The archetypal foundation of biblical leadership is a gradual process of recalibrating and turning our desires and affections away from ourselves, and directing them towards God and others.[127] This involves a process of continually "exposing ourselves to God's Truth and responding to God with it."[128] In addition to the importance of a leader increasing in wisdom and knowledge of God, leadership and disciple-making must also involve the wonderful process of "allowing the peace of Christ to rule in our hearts."[129] And herein resides the delicate balance and interplay between what a leader should *know* (their cognition and beliefs) and what a leader should *do* (their affections and behaviors).

---

[125] Genesis 3:6

[126] The concept of *turned* love was identified in Michael Reeves book *Delighting In The Trinity* (IVP Academic, Downers Grove, IN: 2012), p. 65.

[127] James K.A. Smith. *You Are What You Love*. (Baker Publishing, Grand Rapids, MI: 2016), p. 25.

[128] Clem. November, 2019.

[129] Colossians 3:15

Our affections are shaped by a combination of what we believe in addition to our daily actions and habitual behaviors.[130] Therefore, as a starting point disciple-makers and leaders must likewise embrace the discipline of increasing in Truth and knowledge of God. The leader must be biblically formed and have command of the Word of God as the basis for establishing conviction in their faith in Jesus Christ.[131] Yet we must not stop with "head knowledge." The leader must also be immersed in spiritual practices and virtues that allow them to *train their loves* and "habituate themselves as citizens of the Kingdom of God."[132]

---

[130] Smith, pp. 14-15.
[131] Taylor, pp. 93-94.
[132] Smith, p. 25.

THE ONE THING NECESSARY

"Mary has chosen what is better."
— Luke 10:42

IN THE BEAUTIFUL ACCOUNT OF JESUS at the home of Mary and Martha, Jesus teaches the principle that is the cornerstone of biblical leadership: That Jesus Christ himself is the *unum neccessarum*. The story illustrates the tension that leaders will continually face between the *one and the many.* Although Martha was distracted by *many things*, Mary had established within her heart the *one thing that mattered most.* The biblical method of leadership is therefore portrayed as a constant recalibrating of the affections of the heart and the attention of the mind to the *unum neccessarum*—which is God Himself, revealed in the person of Jesus Christ.[133] This particular gospel narrative also illustrates two very specific and fundamental aspects of leadership.

First, the biblical leader must be immersed in the teachings of Jesus Christ contained within the four gospels.

---

[133] Hebrews 1:3

You must strive to emulate Mary and "sit at the feet of the Lord, listening to what he says."[134] In other words, a biblical leader will be a *learner* at the feet of Jesus. Jesus exemplified the importance of *teaching* to the point of even shaping the very words of his disciple's prayer life.[135] Jesus took special pains to explain difficult Scripture passages for his disciples,[136] and his ability to recall God's Word by memory was constantly impressed upon them.

Additionally, Jesus made it clear that his words would need to "remain in his disciples" in order for them to be effective in spreading the gospel message.[137] After Jesus' disciples had consistently *observed* his commitment to times of daily prayer they said, "Lord, teach us to pray."[138] In other words, Jesus' *demonstration* of prayer was a catalyst to his *teaching on prayer.* Capitalizing on the opportunity when it presented itself, Jesus responded by teaching his disciples a model prayer.[139] By essentially "putting words into their mouths to get them to pray,"[140] Jesus highlighted the significance of a disciple as a *learner* at the feet of a *leader*.

---

[134] Luke 10:38
[135] Matthew 6:9-13
[136] Coleman, p. 65.
[137] John 15:7-8
[138] Luke 11:1
[139] Luke 11:2-4
[140] Coleman, p. 64.

Second, biblical leadership must include developing practices and rituals that open our heart to Jesus.[141] In the account of Mary and Martha, it was the combination of *listening to what Jesus said* in addition to *sitting at his feet* that illustrates Mary's love for Jesus and her heart for discipleship. Because Mary had made Jesus her *unum neccessarum,* the totality of her life began to revolve around him. This is an important implication because it emphasizes the leader's *entire life* is to be submitted to Jesus.[142] Rather than compartmentalizing and inviting Jesus into only fractions of your life, the principle of *unum neccessarum* dictates that every single area of your life is to be brought under the rule and Lordship of Christ.[143]

In the presence of Jesus, Mary was able to *listen to what he said,* and also *watch what he did.* This principle is also beautifully illustrated in Jesus' calling of Levi to *follow him.*[144] The implication is that by *following the Master,* Jesus' disciples and future leaders were constantly in his presence, observing everything that he both *said and did.* This model of "full immersion discipleship" was so effective that in

---

[141] Smith, p. 185.
[142] Wilkins, p. 343.
[143] Wilkins, p. 274.
[144] Luke 5:27-28

Luke's account of this principle in the book of Acts, we should take special note that "when they saw the courage of Peter and John and realized they were unschooled, ordinary men, they were astonished and they took note that these men *had been with Jesus*."[145]

[145] Acts 4:13. My use of italics within this Scripture to highlight that Peter and John had *been in the company of Jesus*.

THE MECHANICS OF BIBLICAL LEADERSHIP

"Be prepared in season and out of season; correct, rebuke and encourage."
— 2 Timothy 4:2

AN ADHERENT OF BIBLICAL LEADERSHIP must ultimately move from theory to application. Therefore, what are the actual "rubber meets the road" mechanics of leading others and making disciples? The first step involves the moment that a leader calls a new believer into fellowship with Jesus and a lifetime of discipleship at the feet of the Master.[146] Inside the Church, mature Christians must be on the active lookout for first time attendees and people new to faith in Jesus. The prescription for bringing new believers into spiritual growth involves men and women mature in their walk with Jesus extending an invitation to those at the inception of the journey. In other words, it takes a leader to disciple another person.

---

146 In the context as being at the "feet of Jesus," Wilkins wrote that, "the Church today is the body of Jesus, and is the particular tool of the discipleship process" (Wilkins, p. 279).

This seemingly simple process is the exact replica of Jesus' method: Our Lord called other people into relationship with him, and invited them to follow his example. Therefore, your first step must always include welcoming others into a personal and loving relationship with Jesus Christ, in addition to the "life-on-life" fellowship that is nurtured between yourself and those whom God has entrusted you to lead.[147]

The next step of the disciple-making process involves bringing new believers into the fellowship and support of a small group. This principle is evidenced in the gospel according to Mark: "Jesus appointed twelve – designating them apostles – that they might *be with him* and that he might send them out to preach and to have authority to drive out demons."[148] In other words, Jesus called his twelve disciples and future leaders into a *personal relationship with him,* and into a *community relationship* with other leaders. This is the essence of the modern day "small group" and "Bible study" community that is so effective in supporting spiritual growth.

---

[147] The relationship between the disciple and disciple-maker should be of the same gender (Mark 6:7; Luke 10:1). I am also reminded of the words of Billy Graham who wrote that, "As Christ's representative in a needy world, demonstrate your new life by your love and concern for others" (from Graham's booklet *Steps To Peace With God,* Billy Graham Evangelistic Association, Minneapolis, MN.).

[148] Mark 3:14-15. My use of italics within this Scripture.

Within the context of the small group, the deeper questions of the Christian faith can be studied and explored. It is significant that within the small group community developed by Jesus, Peter was most comfortable asking Jesus the questions that contributed to the group's collective growth.

The third step of the disciple-making program involves Church attendance. The unity of the body of Christ is essential to the growth of the individual believer.[149] The Church is the embodiment of Christ with his people and is the place where "the Spirit meets, nourishes, transforms, and empowers us" through the corporate practices of worship.[150]

The three-tiered process of leadership and disciple-making now becomes self-evident: A leader *calls* a new believer into a personal relationship with Jesus Christ. This relationship, although deeply intimate with Jesus, is also supported by the "life-on-life" relationship between the leader and their disciple, in addition to the second step of a small group community. The third step is a natural progression and includes a weekly Church service for the purpose of fellowship with other believers, worshiping God, and experiencing "the Spirit and his body, the Church, where Jesus continues to minister to his disciples."[151]

---

[149] Smith, p. 70; Cf; Wilkins p. 278-280.
[150] Smith, p. 70.
[151] Wilkins, p. 279.

SPIRITUAL WEIGHTLIFTING

"I discipline my body like an athlete, training it to do what it should."
— 1 Corinthians 9:27

THE PROCESS OF BIBLICAL LEADERSHIP AND BECOMMING like Jesus is more akin to a fitness program than reading a dense theological book or listening to an encouraging sermon-Podcast on Christian doctrine.[152] In this sense, the spiritual disciplines are the means by which you can begin to experience the transformative power of God's sanctifying grace.[153] The spiritual disciplines provide both *closeness to Jesus* and *conformity to his way of life*. In addition, the disciplines are both personal and interpersonal activities that can be instructed and practiced within the framework of the discipleship program, and subsequently maintained for the remainder of the disciple's lifetime.

---

[152] Smith, p. 65.
[153] Donald S. Whitney, Spiritual Disciplines for the Christian Life, (NavPress: Colorado Springs, CO), p. 9.

The three foundational spiritual disciplines that reside within the biblical leadership program are Bible intake (reading from God's Word), prayer (both individual and corporate), and meditation.[154] These disciplines integrate both the *head* and the *heart* and invite the leader into daily and weekly routines that shape their fundamental desires, which subsequently influence how they move and behave in the world.[155]

A daily period of ten minutes of reading from the Bible (ideally the gospels of Matthew, Mark, Luke, and John) followed by a period of reflection on God's Word will equate to Mary at the feet of Jesus. Allowing the words of Jesus to circulate within your mind will provide greater opportunity for God's Spirit to reveal His Truth to you throughout the day. In addition, reading from God's Word will enhance and support your spiritual discipline of prayer in a profound way. Jesus had every intention that his disciples committed themselves to daily prayer, and his unmistakable expectation for a leader's commitment to a prayerful life is echoed throughout the New Testament.[156]

---

[154] For a complete description and teaching on all of the Spiritual Disciplines, I recommend Whitney's book *Spiritual Disciplines for the Christian Life,* or my book *VICTORY – A Practical Guide to Eternal Fitness,* (Eagle Rise Publishing: Virginia Beach, VA, 2019).

[155] Smith, p. 65.

[156] Colossians 4:2

Meditation on Jesus in silence and solitude provides the much needed space in your life for the Holy Spirit to reveal within your heart what could never be discerned by "flesh and blood."[157] For example, when Peter declared that Jesus was "the Christ, the Son of the Living God," Jesus commended him and acknowledged this revelation was "not achieved by something that he *heard* but rather by what God had done in his *heart*."[158]

You must always remember that your highest potential for leadership and spiritual growth is achieved through the power of the Holy Spirit. In this sense, although time in "life-on-life," small group, and Church attendance is important for a leader, the most important use of your time will always be found within the intimacy of personal fellowship and devotion spent at the feet of the Master himself.

---

[157] Matthew 6:17
[158] Matthew 6:13-20. My use of italics.

PART FOUR

PROFILE OF A LEADER

FOLLOW ME!

"Follow my example."
— 1 Corinthians 11:1

BIBLICAL REVELATION TREATS God's attributes and qualities not in a speculative way, but rather in an objective and practical manner.[159] There is a vital and clear connection between *who God is* and *what God does*. In other words, there is a direct causation between God's attributes and God's actions. In the same manner, as you increase in the likeness and character of Jesus, you will begin to progressively reflect Jesus to those around you.

The following are 24 traits that every biblical leader will demonstrate increasing evidence of. Although not an exhaustive list, these 24 traits serve as foundational to the life of someone desirous of proclaiming with both their words and actions, "Follow my example, even as I follow the example of Christ" (1 Corinthians 11:1).

[159] Millard Erickson, *Christian Theology.* (Baker Academic, Grand Rapids, MI. 2013), p. 270.

COGNITIVE TRAITS:

What a Leader Knows

1. A biblical leader[160] will be equipped with knowledge of prayer, and the power that prayer holds for the forgiveness of sins and healing (James 5:16).

2. The leader will believe that the Bible is the Word of God and is useful for guiding their beliefs and actions. They will have knowledge of God's Word and feel empowered to share it with new believers (2 Timothy 3:16-17; 2 Peter 1:19-21).

3. The leader will understand the arch of the biblical narrative and how the entire Bible both points to and is fulfilled in Jesus Christ (John 5:39-40; Luke 24:27, 44-47).

4. The leader will know the spiritual disciplines, and those specific disciplines best suited for their continued spiritual growth (1 Corinthians 9:24-27).

[160] It should be noted that a *discipled person* is by design also a *disciple-maker* and a *leader*. Therefore, in the list of 24 character traits I use the term *discipled person, leader* and *disciple-maker* nearly interchangeably.

5. A leader will be able to identify their own unique spiritual gifts in addition to helping new believers identify and develop their spiritual gifts and calling (1 Corinthians 12:4-14; 1 Peter 4:10-11).

6. A leader will understand that a person comes into a righteous relationship with God not through work, but by God's grace, through faith in Jesus Christ (Ephesians 2:8-9).

7. A leader will know that all people are loved by God and need Jesus Christ as their Lord and Savior. Their sense of being loved by Jesus will compel them to share the love of Christ with others and "make disciples of all the nations" (Matthew 28:19; John 3:16; 2 John 4:9-10).

8. The leader will understand that the God of the Bible is the One True God, revealed within the Trinity, as the Father, Son, and Holy Spirit (2 Corinthians 13:14; John 20:31).

AFFECTIVE TRAITS:

What a Leader Feels

1. A biblical leader allows for the indwelling power of the Holy Spirit to convict sin in their life. They will be equipped with a gentle yet firm capacity for helping others identify sin in their life, to repent, and to receive the forgiveness of Christ (Acts 2:38).[161]

2. The leader will believe in their heart that Jesus Christ "has the words of eternal life and is the Holy One of God" (John 6:67-29). This conviction will enable the biblical leader to share the good news of God's mercy and love with others.[162]

3. The leader is guided in their desires, thoughts, words, and actions by the indwelling power of the Holy Spirit (Galatians 5:16).

4. The leaders new life in Christ will increasingly manifest itself by their desire and ability to share the love of Christ with others (John 8:31-32; 1 John 2:3-6).[163]

---

[161] Michael Wilkins, *Following the Master.* (Zondervan, Grand Rapids, MI. 1992), p. 120.
[162] Ibid, p. 115.
[163] Ibid, p. 303.

5. The leader will have a love and affection for prayer, and will practice prayer for themselves, other believers, Church leaders, and government leaders. They will invite new believers into prayer within the framework of "life-on-life" fellowship, small group community, and corporate worship of God at a local Church (1 Thessalonians 5:17; Colossians 1:9).[164]

6. The leaders heart for their brother and sister will enable a special capacity to call others into fellowship with Jesus and a lifetime of discipleship at the feet of the Master (Luke 10:39).

7. The leader will be part of a local gathering of fellow Christians where they will worship God for what He has done both within their individual life, and the entire Body of Christ (Acts 2:42-47; Psalm 95:1-2).

8. The leader will offer their time for the purpose of discipling new believers, sharing God's Word, and serving within their faith community (Colossians 3:17; Matthew 28:19-20; 1 John 4:10-12).

---

[164] Wilkins p. 304.

EFFECTIVE TRAITS:

What a Leader Does

1. The biblical leader believes that Jesus Christ is Lord, which is evidenced by their obedience to His commands (1 John 2:3-6; John 14:15).

2. The leader will prioritize time alone with God each day for the purpose of the spiritual disciplines to include reading the Bible, memorizing Scripture, prayer, and meditation (Psalm 1:2-3, 119:7; Colossians 4:2).

3. A leader will treat their body as a temple, which will be demonstrated in a commitment to daily exercise including a combination of functional movement, constant variance, and high intensity. They will maintain good nutritional standards, abstain from all narcotics, and maintain self-control in the consumption of alcohol (1 Corinthians 6:19; Romans 13:3).

4. A leader actively and enthusiastically encourages new believers to live out God's purposes for their life (Ecclesiastes 3:1; 1 Peter 2:9; Jeremiah 29:11).

5. A leader meets on a regular (weekly) basis with other Christians for the purpose of studying God's Word, and applying God's Word within their lives. They will invite new believers into fellowship to include "life-on-life," small group, and corporate Church attendance (Hebrews 10:24-25; Matthew 18:20).
6. A leader does not have sexual relationships that are contrary to biblical teaching (1 Corinthians 6:18, 7:2; Hebrews 13:4).
7. The leader keeps their composure and *Shalom* when other people or life circumstances are difficult or challenging (James 1:2-4; Philippians 4:4-7).
8. A leader is a force multiplier. Their positive mental attitude, sense of optimism and encouragement of others is evident in everything that they say and do (2 Numbers 13:30; Corinthians 3:11; 1 Thessalonians 5:11).

EPILOGUE

BEING A GOOD SOLDIER

EPILOGUE

"I have given you an example."
— John 13:15

WHEN IT IS ALL BOILED DOWN, those of us seeking to *fight well, finish the race, and keep the faith* must be prepared for the inevitable assignment of leadership that God has in store for us.[(ii)] As a *good soldier of Jesus Christ,* your life will become increasingly conformed to his character and likeness as you are shaped by the indwelling power of the Holy Spirit.[165] Soon enough, the practical outworking in your life of the deeper realities of the Spirit will begin to *reflect* and *connect* God to those around you.

Every facet of your life has the potential to demonstrate the transformative power of the Gospel in real-time to those people within your circle of influence. Therefore, as you answer the call to self-mastery in the service of others, you must remain keenly aware that people will begin to follow you, even as you follow Christ.[166] In other words, everything

---

[165] 2 Corinthians 3:18
[166] 1 Corinthians 11:1

you say and do must emulate an example worthy of being followed. This is due to the fact that those people who follow you will begin to imitate those things that they hear and see in you.[167]

Jesus Christ employed this demonstrative method of leadership in such a pronounced way that we must strongly consider the implied requirement to obey and follow his example. Jesus never asked anyone to do or be anything that he did not first demonstrate, reveal, model, and perfectly exhibit in his own life.[168]

Everything that Jesus said and did was a lesson in leadership. Since Jesus' disciples were with him practically every waking moment of their day, they were experiencing first-hand the most perfect model of "leadership by example and from the front" that the world has ever seen. Slowly but surely, the disciples began to align their thinking, speaking and behavior into harmony with Jesus.[169]

This observation seems to prove that given time, it is possible through the biblical method of leadership to impart your way of living to those people whom God will entrust you with. The key insight is that although it can be good to tell people what to do, it is *infinitely better to model it*

---

[167] Philippians 4:9
[168] Robert Coleman. *The Master Plan of Evangelism.* (Grand Rapids, MI. Revell Press, 1993), p. 68.
[169] Acts 4:13

for them. People are drawn to leaders who demonstrate a transformed way of life, not just an explanation of what it could potentially look like.

The archetype of demonstrative leadership is unique to the Bible, and will make you extremely vulnerable. You are not perfect as our Lord Jesus Christ was. Those persons enlisted as *good soldiers* will soon discover their many shortcomings. However, even these shortcomings can serve the Kingdom of God, for it will allow your followers to see a courageous readiness to confess mistakes and a personal responsibility for the consequences of misplaced priorities and flawed behaviors.[170]

The struggle and challenge of your increasing spiritual maturity need not impede your leadership ability, when shining through you is the transparency of a good soldier dedicated to following Jesus, and a warrior after God's own heart.

[170] Coleman, p. 68.

BENEDICTION

THINKING RIGHT ABOUT GOD

RIGHTEOUS THOUGHTS

"Let God transform you into a new person by changing the way you think."
— Romans 12:2 (NLT)

THE THOUGHTS IN YOUR MIND about God are the most important thing about you.[171] In other words, if you think incorrectly about God, it is not God who changes. You change for the better or worse and in direct proportion to your better or worse thoughts about God.

Being a *good soldier* and *fighting well, finishing the race, and keeping the faith* are all unequivocally dependent upon your ability to first think rightly about God.

For the purposes of concluding this book, I encourage you to embrace three foundational ideas about God:

[171] The great Christian mystic A.W. Tozer said that, "What comes into our mind when we think about God is the most important thing about us."

1. *God is entirely devoted to your spiritual advancement.*[172]
2. *When you trust God to lead you, He will trust you to lead others.*[173]
3. *God is good.*[174]

Having faith in the idea that God is good, devoted to your advancement, and desirous of enabling you to lead yourself and others, is tantamount to your success, fulfillment, and happiness. Your entire outlook on life will be instantly changed when your heart knows that God, although exalted in power and majesty, is eager to be your friend, and that He only wants what is best for you.

[172] Jeremiah 29:11 promises that the plans God has for you are meant to prosper you, to give you hope in your endeavors and a bright future.
[173] 2 Samuel 3:1 explains that King David's faith in God and obedience to Him enabled David to become stronger and more capable of leading others both in peacetime and in war.
[174] James 1:17 states that every good and perfect gift comes from God, and in Mark 10:18 Jesus Christ said that only God is good.

SCRIPTURE INDEX

INTRODUCTION

1. "God testified concerning him: 'I have found David son of Jesse, a man after my own heart; he will do everything I want him to do'" (Acts 13:22).

2. "Although people look at the outward appearance, the LORD looks at the heart" (1 Samuel 16:7).

3. "For although they knew God, they neither glorified him as God nor gave thanks to him, but their thinking became futile and their foolish hearts were darkened. Although they claimed to be wise, they became fools and exchanged the glory of the immortal God for images made to look like a mortal human being and birds and animals and reptiles. They exchanged the truth about God for a lie, and worshiped and served created things rather than the Creator – who is forever praised" (Romans 1:21-23; 25).

4. "When the people saw that Moses was so long in coming down from the mountain, they gathered around Aaron and said, 'Come, make us gods who will go before us. As for this fellow Moses who brought us up out of Egypt, we don't know what has happened to him.'

   Aaron answered them, 'Take off the gold earrings that your wives, your sons and your daughters are wearing, and bring them to me.' So all the people took off their earrings and brought them to Aaron. He took what they handed him and made it into an idol cast in the shape of a calf, fashioning it with a tool. Then they said, 'These are your gods, Israel, who brought you up out of Egypt.'

When Aaron saw this, he built an altar in front of the calf and announced, 'Tomorrow there will be a festival to the Lord.' So the next day the people rose early and sacrificed burnt offerings and presented fellowship offerings. Afterward they sat down to eat and drink and got up to indulge in revelry.

Then the Lord said to Moses, 'Go down, because your people, whom you brought up out of Egypt, have become corrupt. They have been quick to turn away from what I commanded them and have made themselves an idol cast in the shape of a calf. They have bowed down to it and sacrificed to it and have said, 'These are your gods, Israel, who brought you up out of Egypt'" (Exodus 32:1-8).

5. Non-biblical reference.

6. "No one serving as a soldier gets entangled in civilian affairs, but rather tries to please his commanding officer" (2 Timothy 2:4).

   "Finally, be strong in the Lord and in his mighty power. Put on the full armor of God, so that you can take your stand against the devil's schemes. For our struggle is not against flesh and blood, but against the rulers, against the authorities, against the powers of this dark world and against the spiritual forces of evil in the heavenly realms. Therefore, put on the full armor of God, so that when the day of evil comes, you may be able to stand your ground, and after you have done everything, to stand. Stand firm then, with the belt of truth buckled around your waist, with the breastplate of righteousness in place, and with your feet fitted with the readiness that comes from the gospel of peace. In addition to all this, take up the shield of faith, with which you can extinguish all the flaming arrows of the evil one. Take the helmet of salvation and the sword of the Spirit, which is the word of God" (Ephesians 6:10-17).

7. "I have fought the good fight, I have finished the race, I have kept the faith" (2 Timothy 4:7).

PART ONE

8. "Stand firm then, with the belt of truth buckled around your waist, with the breastplate of righteousness in place, and with your feet fitted with the readiness that comes from the gospel of peace. In addition to all this, take up the shield of faith, with which you can extinguish all the flaming arrows of the evil one. Take the helmet of salvation and the sword of the Spirit, which is the word of God" (Ephesians 6:14-17).

9. "The one who does what is sinful is of the devil, because the devil has been sinning from the beginning. The reason the Son of God appeared was to destroy the devil's work" (1 John 3:8).

10. "Through death Jesus destroyed him that had the power of death, that is, the devil" (Hebrews 2:14b). Reference creed of the U.S. Army Soldier.

11. "I keep asking that the God of our Lord Jesus Christ, the glorious Father, may give you the Spirit of wisdom and revelation, so that you may know him better" (Ephesians 1:17).

12. Non-biblical reference.

13. “Some trust in chariots and some in horses, but we trust in the name of the Lord our God” (Psalm 20:7).

14. “The Lord said to Gideon, ‘You have too many men. I cannot deliver Midian into their hands, or Israel would boast against me and say, ‘My own strength has saved me’” (Judges 7:2).

15. “So Gideon took the men down to the water. There the LORD told him, ‘Separate those who lap the water with their tongues as a dog laps from those who kneel down to drink’” (Judges 7:5).

16. “Where there is no vision, the people perish; but blessed is the one who heeds wisdom’s instruction” (Proverbs 29:18).

17. “When I and all who are with me blow our trumpets, then from all around the camp blow yours and shout, ‘For the LORD and for Gideon’” (Judges 7:18).

18. “When the three hundred trumpets sounded, the Lord caused the men throughout the camp to turn on each other with their swords. The army fled to Beth Shittah toward Zererah as far as the border of Abel Meholah near Tabbath” (Judges 7:22).

19. Judges 7:18.

20. “The LORD will grant that the enemies who rise up against you will be defeated before you. They will come at you from one direction but flee from you in seven” (Deuteronomy 28:7).

21. “But David went back and forth from Saul to tend his father’s sheep at Bethlehem. For forty days the Philistine came forward every morning and evening and took his stand.

    Now Jesse said to his son David, ‘Take this ephah of roasted grain and these ten loaves of bread for your brothers and hurry to their camp. Take along these ten cheeses to the commander of their unit. See how your brothers are and bring back some assurance from them. They are with Saul and all the men of Israel in the Valley of Elah, fighting against the Philistines'" (1 Samuel 17:15-19).

22. "I have seen a son of Jesse of Bethlehem who knows how to play the lyre. He is a brave man and a warrior. He speaks well and is a fine looking man, and the LORD is with him" (1 Samuel 16:18).

23. "David left his things with the keeper of supplies, ran to the battle lines and asked his brothers how they were" (1 Samuel 17:22).

24. "On hearing the Philistine's words, Saul and all the Israelites were dismayed and terrified" (1 Samuel 17:22).

25. "David asked the men standing near him, 'What will be done for the man who kills this Philistine and removes this disgrace from Israel? Who is this uncircumcised Philistine that he should defy the armies of the living God?'" (1 Samuel 17:26).

26. "When Eliab, David's oldest brother, heard him speaking with the men, he burned with anger at him and asked, 'Why have you come down here? And with whom did you leave those few sheep in the wilderness? I know how conceited you are and how wicked your heart is; you came down only to watch the battle'" (1 Samuel 17:28).

27. "The LORD who rescued me from the paw of the lion and the paw of the bear will rescue me from the hand of this Philistine" (1 Samuel 17:37).

28. "Not by might, nor by power, but by my Spirit, says the LORD Almighty" (Zechariah 4:6).

29. "All those gathered here will know that it is not by sword or spear that the LORD saves; for the battle is the LORD's, and he will give all of you into our hands" (1 Samuel 17:47).

30. "Reaching into his bag and taking out a stone, he slung it and struck the Philistine on the forehead. The stone sank into his forehead, and he fell facedown on the ground" (1 Samuel 17:49).

31. "He chose David his servant and took him from the sheep pens; from tending the sheep he brought him to be the shepherd of his people" (Psalm 78:78-71).

32. "The thief comes only to steal and kill and destroy; I have come that they may have life, and have it to the full" (John 10:10).

33. "For our struggle is not against flesh and blood, but against the rulers, against the authorities, against the powers of this dark world and against the spiritual forces of evil in the heavenly realms" (Ephesians 6:16).

34. "His master replied, 'Well done, good and faithful servant! You have been faithful with a few things; I will put you in charge of many things. Come and share your master's happiness!'" (Matthew 25:23).

35. "He that dwells in the secret place of the Most High will rest in the shadow of the Almighty" (Psalm 91:1—The remainder of the entire Psalm elaborates on this principle).

36. "You intended to harm me, but God intended it for good to accomplish what is now being done, the saving of many

lives" (Genesis 50:20).

37. "After fasting forty days and forty nights, Jesus was hungry" (Matthew 4:2).

38. "In addition to all this, take up the shield of faith, with which you can extinguish all the flaming arrows of the evil one" (Ephesians 6:16).

39. "The tempter came to him and said, 'If you are the Son of God, tell these stones to become bread'" (Matthew 4:3).

40. "And Jesus grew in wisdom and stature, and in favor with God and man" (Luke 2:52).

41. "Then God said, 'Let us make mankind in our image, in our likeness, so that they may rule over the fish in the sea and the birds in the sky, over the livestock and all the wild animals, and over all the creatures that move along the ground'" (Genesis 1:26).

42. "Take the helmet of salvation and the sword of the Spirit, which is the word of God" (Ephesians 6:17).

43. "Jesus answered, 'It is written: 'Man shall not live on bread alone, but on every word that comes from the mouth of God'" (Matthew 4:4).

44. "Then the devil took him to the holy city and had him stand on the highest point of the temple. 'If you are the Son of God,' he said, 'throw yourself down. For it is written:

    'He will command his angels concerning you, and they will lift you up in their hands, so that you will not strike your foot against a stone.' Jesus answered him, 'It is also written: 'Do not put the Lord your God to the test'" (Matthew 4:5-7).

45. "And my God will meet all your needs according to the riches

of his glory in Christ Jesus" (Philippians 4:19).

46. "'All this I will give you,' he said, 'if you will bow down and worship me'" (Matthew 4:9).

47. "Catch for us the foxes, the little foxes that ruin the vineyards, our vineyards that are in bloom" (Song of Solomon 2:15).

48. "Jesus said to him, 'Away from me, Satan! For it is written: 'Worship the Lord your God, and serve him only'" (Matthew 4:10).

49. "In Jesus Christ you have been brought to fullness" (Colossians 2:10).

50. "The LORD is a warrior, the LORD is His name" (Exodus 15:3).

51. "Through you we push back our enemies; through your name we trample our foes" (Psalm 44:5).

52. "Before I formed you in the womb I knew you, before you were born I set you apart; I appointed you as a prophet to the nations" (Jeremiah 1:5).

53. "Stand firm then, with the belt of truth buckled around your waist, with the breastplate of righteousness in place, and with your feet fitted with the readiness that comes from the gospel of peace. In addition to all this, take up the shield of faith, with which you can extinguish all the flaming arrows of the evil one. Take the helmet of salvation and the sword of the Spirit, which is the word of God" (Ephesians 6:14-17).

PART TWO

54. "Through death Jesus destroyed him that had the power of death, that is, the devil" (Hebrews 2:14b).

55. "Trust in the LORD with all your heart and lean not on your own understanding; in all your ways submit to him, and he will make your paths straight" (Proverbs 3:5-6).

56. "Where there is no vision, the people perish; but blessed is the one who heeds wisdom's instruction" (Proverbs 29:18).

57. "Do not be wise in your own eyes; fear the LORD and shun evil" (Proverbs 3:7).

58. "And the surpassing greatness of God for us who believe" (Ephesians 1:19).

59. "Such 'wisdom' does not come down from heaven but is earthly, unspiritual, demonic. For where you have envy and selfish ambition, there you find disorder and every evil practice" (James 3:5-6).

60. James 3:5-6

61. "I pray that the eyes of your heart may be enlightened in order that you may know the hope to which he has called you, the riches of his glorious inheritance in his holy people" (Ephesians 1:18).

62. "So God created mankind in his own image, in the image of God he created them; male and female he created them" (Genesis 1:27).

63. "Now this is eternal life: that they know you, the only true God, and Jesus Christ, whom you have sent" (John 17:3).

64. "But their minds were made dull, for to this day the same veil remains when the old covenant is read. It has not been removed, because only in Christ is it taken away. Even to this day when Moses is read, a veil covers their hearts"

(2 Corinthians 3:14-15).

65. Non-biblical reference.

66. Non-biblical reference.

67. "For the flesh desires what is contrary to the Spirit, and the Spirit what is contrary to the flesh. They are in conflict with each other, so that you are not to do whatever you want" (Galatians 5:17).

68. "But as for you, the LORD took you and brought you out of the iron-smelting furnace, out of Egypt, to be the people of his inheritance, as you now are" (Deuteronomy 4:20).

69. "I prayed to the LORD and said, "Sovereign LORD, do not destroy your people, your own inheritance that you redeemed by your great power and brought out of Egypt with a mighty hand" (Deuteronomy 9:26).

70. "This, then, is how you should pray: 'Our Father in heaven, hallowed be your name'" (Matthew 6:9).

71. "I keep asking that the God of our Lord Jesus Christ, the glorious Father, may give you the Spirit of wisdom and revelation, in the knowledge of Him" (Ephesians 1:17).

72. "All I have is yours, and all you have is mine. And glory has come to me through them" (John 17:10).

73. "While Aaron was speaking to the whole Israelite community, they looked toward the desert, and there was the glory of the LORD appearing in the cloud" (Exodus 16:10).

74. "And the surpassing greatness of God for us who believe" (Ephesians 1:19).

PART THREE

75. Non-biblical reference.

76. Non-biblical reference.

77. "The LORD had said to Abram, 'Go from your country, your people and your father's household to the land I will show you'" (Genesis 12:1).

78. "By faith Abraham, when called to go to a place he would later receive as his inheritance, obeyed and went, even though he did not know where he was going" (Hebrews 11:8).

79. "Is it a time for you yourselves to be living in your paneled houses, while this house remains a ruin?" (Haggai 1:4).

80. "I will make you into a great nation, and I will bless you; I will make your name great, and you will be a blessing. I will bless those who bless you, and whoever curses you I will curse; and all peoples on earth will be blessed through you" (Genesis 12:2-3).

81. Refer to footnote on page 40.

82. "Going on from there, he saw two other brothers, James son of Zebedee and his brother John. They were in a boat with their father Zebedee, preparing their nets. Jesus called them, and immediately they left the boat and their father and followed him" (Matthew 4:21-22).

83. "In the past, while Saul was king over us, you were the one who led Israel on their military campaigns. And the LORD said to you, 'You will shepherd my people Israel, and you will become their ruler'" (2 Samuel 5:2).

84. "Therefore go and make disciples of all nations, baptizing

them in the name of the Father and of the Son and of the Holy Spirit, and teaching them to obey everything I have commanded you. And surely I am with you always, to the very end of the age" (Matthew 28:19-20. My use of italics and exegesis within the brackets to emphasize Jesus' command for both *leading others* and *disciple-making*).

85. "But seek first his kingdom and his righteousness, and all these things will be given to you as well" (Matthew 6:33).

86. Non-biblical reference.

87. "The acts of the flesh are obvious: sexual immorality, impurity and debauchery idolatry and witchcraft; hatred, discord, jealousy, fits of rage, selfish ambition, dissensions, factions and envy; drunkenness, orgies, and the like. I warn you, as I did before, that those who live like this will not inherit the kingdom of God" (Galatians 5:19-21).

88. "Therefore, if anyone is in Christ, the new creation has come: The old has gone, the new is here!" (2 Corinthians 5:17).

89. "But we all, with open face beholding as in a glass the glory of the Lord, are changed into the same image from glory to glory, even as by the Spirit of the Lord" (2 Corinthians 3:18).

90. Non-biblical reference.

91. Non-biblical reference.

92. "Follow me, even as I follow Christ" (1 Corinthians 11:1).

93. Non-biblical reference.

94. Non-biblical reference.

95. "Therefore go and make disciples of all nations, baptizing them in the name of the Father and of the Son and of the

Holy Spirit, and teaching them to obey everything I have commanded you" (Matthew 28:19).

96. Non-biblical reference.

97. Non-biblical reference.

98. Non-biblical reference.

99. Non-biblical reference.

100. Non-biblical reference.

101. Non-biblical reference.

102. Non-biblical reference.

103. "If you love me, obey my commandments" (John 14:15).

104. "Join with me in suffering, like a good soldier of Christ Jesus" (2 Timothy 2:3).

105. "But you will receive power when the Holy Spirit comes on you; and you will be my witnesses in Jerusalem, and in all Judea and Samaria, and to the ends of the earth" (Acts 1:8).

106. "Now teach these truths to other trustworthy people who will be able to pass them on to others" (2 Timothy 2:2 - New Living Translation).

107. "Again Jesus said, "Peace be with you! As the Father has sent me, I am sending you" (John 20:21).

108. "In everything set them an example by doing what is good. In your teaching show integrity, seriousness" (Titus 2:7).

109. "The student is not above the teacher, but everyone who is fully trained will be like their teacher" (Luke 6:40).

110. "You became imitators of us and of the Lord, for you welcomed

the message in the midst of severe suffering with the joy given by the Holy Spirit. And so you became a model to all the believers in Macedonia and Achaia" (1 Thessalonians 1:6-7. My use of italics and paraphrasing within this Scripture).

111. "If you declare with your mouth, "Jesus is Lord," and believe in your heart that God raised him from the dead, you will be saved" (Romans 10:9).

112. Non-biblical reference.

113. Non-biblical reference.

114. "The apostles performed many signs and wonders among the people. And all the believers used to meet together in Solomon's Colonnade" (Acts 5:12).

115. "When Jesus had called the Twelve together, he gave them power and authority to drive out all demons and to cure diseases, and he sent them out to proclaim the Kingdom of God and to heal the sick" (Luke 9:1-2).

116. "All of them were filled with the Holy Spirit and began to speak in other tongues as the Spirit enabled them" (Acts 2:4).

117. "After this the Lord appointed seventy-two others and sent them two by two ahead of him to every town and place where he was about to go" (Luke 10:1).

118. Non-biblical reference.

119. Non-biblical reference.

120. Non-biblical reference.

121. "Jesus replied: 'Love the Lord your God with all your heart and with all your soul and with all your mind. And the second is like it: 'Love your neighbor as yourself'" (Matthew 22:37-39).

122. "When they saw the courage of Peter and John and realized that they were unschooled, ordinary men, they were astonished and they took note that these men had been with Jesus" (Acts 4:13).

123. "Not a word from their mouth can be trusted; their heart is filled with malice. Their throat is an open grave; with their tongues they tell lies" (Psalm 5:9).

124. "Treacherous, rash, conceited, lovers of pleasure rather than lovers of God." (2 Timothy 3:4).

125. "When the woman saw that the fruit of the tree was good for food and pleasing to the eye, and also desirable for gaining wisdom, she took some and ate it. She also gave some to her husband, who was with her, and he ate it" (Genesis 3:6).

126. Non-biblical reference.

127. Non-biblical reference.

128. Non-biblical reference.

129. "Let the peace of Christ rule in your hearts, since as members of one body you were called to peace. And be thankful" (Colossians 3:15).

130. Non-biblical reference.

131. Non-biblical reference.

132. Non-biblical reference.

133. "The Son is the radiance of God's glory and the exact representation of his being, sustaining all things by his powerful word. After he had provided purification for sins, he sat down at the right hand of the Majesty in heaven" (Hebrews 1:3).

134. "As Jesus and his disciples were on their way, he came to a village where a woman named Martha opened her home to him" (Luke 10:38).

135. "This, then, is how you should pray: 'Our Father in heaven, hallowed be your name, your kingdom come, your will be done, on earth as it is in heaven. Give us today our daily bread. And forgive us our debts, as we also have forgiven our debtors. And lead us not into temptation, but deliver us from the evil one'" (Matthew 6:9-13).

136. Non-biblical reference.

137. "If you remain in me and my words remain in you, ask whatever you wish, and it will be done for you" (John 15:7).

138. "One day Jesus was praying in a certain place. When he finished, one of his disciples said to him, 'Lord, teach us to pray, just as John taught his disciples'" (Luke 11:1).

139. "He said to them, when you pray, say: 'Father, hallowed be your name, your kingdom come'" (Luke 11:2).

140. Non-biblical reference.

141. Non-biblical reference.

142. Non-biblical reference.

143. Non-biblical reference.

144. "After this, Jesus went out and saw a tax collector by the name of Levi sitting at his tax booth. 'Follow me,' Jesus said to him" (Luke 5:27).

145. "When they saw the courage of Peter and John and realized that they were unschooled, ordinary men, they were astonished

and they took note that these men had been with Jesus" (Acts 4:13).

146. Non-biblical reference.

147. Non-biblical reference.

148. "He appointed twelve that they might be with him and that he might send them out to preach" (Mark 3:14).

149. Non-biblical reference.

150. Non-biblical reference.

151. Non-biblical reference.

152. Non-biblical reference.

153. Non-biblical reference.

154. Non-biblical reference.

155. Non-biblical reference.

156. "Devote yourselves to prayer, being watchful and thankful" (Colossians 4:2).

157. "Jesus replied, 'Blessed are you, Simon son of Jonah, for this was not revealed to you by flesh and blood, but by my Father in heaven'" (Matthew 6:17).

158. "When Jesus came to the region of Caesarea Philippi, he asked his disciples, 'Who do people say the Son of Man is?' Simon Peter answered, 'You are the Messiah, the Son of the living God.' Jesus replied, 'Blessed are you, Simon son of

Jonah, for this was not revealed to you by flesh and blood, but by my Father in heaven'" (Matthew 6:13, 16-17).

PART FOUR

159. Non-biblical reference.
160. Non-biblical reference.
161. Non-biblical reference.
162. Non-biblical reference.
163. Non-biblical reference.
164. Non-biblical reference.

EPILOGUE

165. "And we all, with unveiled face, beholding the glory of the Lord, are being transformed into the same image from one degree of glory to another. For this comes from the Lord who is the Spirit" (2 Corinthians 3:18).
166. "Follow my example, as I follow the example of Christ" (1 Corinthians 11:1).
167. "Whatever you have learned or received or heard from me, or seen in me—put it into practice. And the God of peace will be with you" (Philippians 4:9).
168. Non-biblical reference.
169. "When they saw the courage of Peter and John and realized that they were unschooled, ordinary men, they were astonished and they took note that these men had been with Jesus" (Acts

4:13).

170. Non-biblical reference.

BENEDICTION

171. Non-biblical reference.

172. "'For I know the plans I have for you,' declares the LORD, 'plans to prosper you and not to harm you, plans to give you hope and a future'" (Jeremiah 29:11).

173. "The war between the house of Saul and the house of David lasted a long time. David grew stronger and stronger, while the house of Saul grew weaker and weaker" (2 Samuel 3:1).

174. "Every good and perfect gift is from above, coming down from the Father of the heavenly lights, who does not change like shifting shadows" (James 1:17).

BIBLIOGRAPHY

1. Coleman, Robert. *The Master Plan of Evangelism*. Grand Rapids, MI. Revell Books, 1972.

2. Elwell, Walter. "Wisdon, Wisdom Literature." Pages 2149 – 2150 in *The Encyclopedia of the Bible*. Grand Rapids, MI. Baker House Book, 1988.

3. Erickson, Millard. *Christian Theology*. Grand Rapids, MI. Baker Academic, 2013.

4. Kolenda, Christopher. *Leadership: The Warriors Art*. Golden, CO. Army War College Foundations Press, 2001.

5. Morley, Patrick. *How God Makes Men*. New York, NY. Crown Publishing, 2013.

6. Redpath, Alan. *The Making of a Man of God*. Grand Rapids, MI. Baker Publishing, 1962.

7. Smith, James. *You Are What You Love*. Grand Rapids, MI. Baker Publishing, 2016.

8. Taylor, Rick. *The Anatomy of a Disciple*. Columbia, SC. Well Community Church, 2013.

9. Tozer, A. W. *The Knowledge of the Holy.* New York, NY. Harper Collins, 1961.

10. Whitney, Donald. *Spiritual Disciplines for the Christian Life.* Colorado Springs, CO. NavPress, 2014.

11. Wilkins, Michael. *Following the Master.* Grand Rapids, MI. Zondervan, 1992.

ENDNOTES

i. I am deeply indebted to the brilliant minds of A.W. Tozer and Alan Redpath for their significant contribution to shaping my thoughts about God and the biblical model of leadership demonstrated in the life of King David. Redpath's bibilical theology on the life of King David in his masterful book *The Making of a Man of God* (Baker Publishing, 1962) significantly shaped my thinking, framing, and conceptualization of the section of my book on *the true cost of leadership.* Any serious student of the Bible must invest in careful study of the theological contributions and exegetical excellence of Tozer and Redpath. With the exception of the Bible, their combined work is the most profound and soul shaping I have ever encountered.

ii. The magnificent work of Robert Coleman and his book *The Master Plan of Evangelism* (Grand Rapids, MI. Revell Press, 1993) significantly shaped my understanding of Jesus' method of evangelism and discipleship, and the greater implications this has for the archetype of demonstrative leadership. The section in Coleman's book on Demonstration (pp. 63-69) helped me frame and conceptualize my argument to the Epilogue of my book.

ALSO FROM BESTSELLING AUTHOR GREG AMUNDSON

Greg Amundson's effective guides to functional fitness, nutrition, goal-setting, pain tolerance, honing purpose and focus, and exerting control over your mental state are designed to help meet any challenge. Packed with practical advice, vetted training methods, and Amundson's guided workout programs, *Firebreather Fitness* is a must-have resource for athletes, coaches, law enforcement and military professionals, and anyone interested in pursuing the high-performance life. Includes a foreword from *New York Times* bestselling author Mark Divine.

The *Warrior and The Monk* tells the extraordinary story of a young warrior who seeks the counsel of a wise monk on the universal quest to find true happiness. This is Greg Amundson's #1 Amazon multi-category bestselling book.

Greg Amundson's book *VICTORY* offers people of all faiths powerful strategies and practical guidelines for bringing health, happiness, fitness, and purpose into their lives and the lives of others. Renowned for his ability to merge fitness and faith, Greg offers a proven methodology for establishing life-affirming beliefs, understanding Divine wisdom, tapping into the power of prayer, integrating physical fitness with spiritual practice, and optimizing the power of mental and physical nutrition.

In a unique and groundbreaking new voice, Greg Amundson merges biblical truth with modern day lessons on leadership, positive psychology, and the warrior spirit. Each day of the year, you will be scripturally guided through the key principles and teachings from the Bible, resulting in a more intimate relationship with God and greater understanding of His Word. Greg's message will help you internalize disciplined practices and ways of thinking that are central to developing your full potential, and achieving your greatest dreams and goals. Greg's integration of the Mind, Body, and Spirit offers a unique perspective to keep you thriving in all aspects of your life.

ABOUT THE AUTHOR

A graduate of the University of California at Santa Cruz, Greg Amundson has spent nearly twenty years in warrior professions to include assignments as a Special Weapons and Tactics Team Operator (SWAT) and Sniper in Santa Cruz County, a Captain in the United States Army, a Special Agent with the Drug Enforcement Administration (DEA) on the Southwest Border and an Agent on the highly effective Border Enforcement Security Taskforce (BEST) Team.

In addition to his extensive government work, Greg is recognized as a thought leader in the field of integrated wellness practices, and is a prolific author and speaker whose message has positively influenced the lives of thousands of spiritual seekers. A former owner of the nations first CrossFit gym, Greg has traveled around the world teaching functional fitness and self-mastery principles for over nineteen years.

Greg is a Krav Maga Black Belt and honor graduate of the Los Angeles Police Department Handgun Instructor School (HITS). Greg currently serves as a Reserve Peace Officer and Law Enforcement Chaplain in Santa Cruz. Greg is also a graduate student at Western Seminary in San Jose, CA., a four-time #1 Amazon bestselling author, and a founding member of the Eagle Rise Speakers Bureau and Eagle Rise Publishing, which has produced numerous bestselling books.

Connect with Greg at www.GregoryAmundson.com.

KEYNOTES AND SEMINARS

Greg Amundson is one of North America's most electric, encouraging, and motivating professional speakers. Greg has logged more than 10,000 hours of dynamic public speaking on topics including leadership, intrinsic motivation, holistic wellness practices, functional fitness, warrior spirit, and God's Love. Greg speaks around the Country to Law Enforcement Departments on integrating disciplined warrior practices to foster increased Officer Safety while simultaneously generating stronger community relationships. A plank owner of the highly regarded Eagle Rise Speakers Bureau, Greg is renowned for his ability to transcend boundaries and speak to the heart of Spirituality. His use of captivating storytelling results in a profound and transformational learning experience.

To book Greg Amundson at your next conference or in-house event please visit www.GregoryAmundson.com.

Made in the USA
Middletown, DE
06 August 2020

14413234R00092